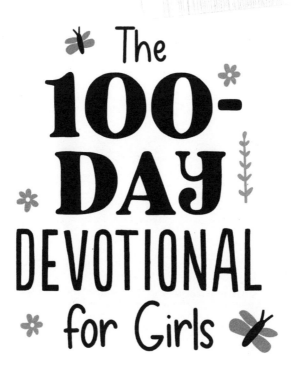

The
100-
DAY
DEVOTIONAL
for Girls

The 100-DAY DEVOTIONAL for Girls

JEAN FISCHER

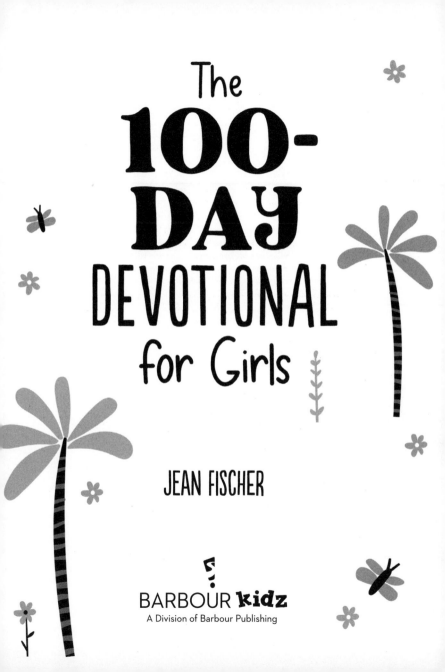

BARBOUR **kidz**
A Division of Barbour Publishing

Print ISBN 978-1-63609-575-2

Published by Barbour Publishing, Inc., 1810 Barbour Drive, Uhrichsville, Ohio 44683, www.barbourbooks.com

Our mission is to inspire the world with the life-changing message of the Bible.

Member of the
Evangelical Christian
Publishers Association

Printed in China.

001570   0523   HA

WHAT IS A "DEVOTiON"?

Maybe you've heard the word *devotion*, but you aren't sure what it means. A devotion is a special kind of reading that leads you nearer to God. The 100 devotions in this book are about things that matter to you—things like kindness, friends, love, joy, talent, courage, faith. . . As you read and think about each devotion, you will discover that you can always trust in God's love. You will learn what He expects from you; and as you grow nearer to Him, you will want to live in ways that please Him.

Read and think about the following scripture. Then use the prayer starter to begin your quiet time talking with God.

❋

*"You will look for Me and find Me, when
you look for Me with all your heart."*
JEREMIAH 29:13

Dear God, I know You are here
with me. Let's talk awhile. . .

MY HiDDEN HEART

When God made your body, He gave it a heart. Your heart is a muscle about the size of your fist. God put it exactly where He wanted it, inside your chest, almost in the middle, between your lungs. The main purpose of your heart muscle is to pump blood throughout your whole body. The blood carries oxygen and other important elements to every body part, and that's what keeps you alive. You probably don't notice, or even think about, your heart beating all day, every day, keeping you alive. A beating heart is one of many blessings God provides us that we take for granted—it seems so ordinary we don't appreciate how amazing it is.

God gave you another kind of heart. It's not one you can see on an X-ray or something a surgeon can touch performing an operation. This kind of heart is tucked deep inside you in a hidden place only God can see. It's the part of you that holds your emotions, feelings, thoughts, and decisions. It's where your conscience is—the part that knows right from wrong.

When your hidden heart is right with God, you feel good about the decisions you make and how you act toward others. But when you act in ways that displease God, your hidden heart makes you feel unsettled. It's like God's voice whispering to you in there, "Are you sure that was the right thing to do?"

You learn about God by reading your Bible and thinking about its words. The more you learn about God, the easier it becomes to know right from wrong. The Bible holds everything you need to discover what it means to follow God and please Him. Bible stories about people are examples that can help you learn the right way to live. What you learn from the Bible is like food for your hidden heart. It fills it up with God's love. And it's God's love that makes your heart healthy and strong.

✺

And so let us come near to God with a true heart full of faith. Our hearts must be made clean from guilty feelings.
HEBREWS 10:22

Dear God, I want my hidden heart to be right with You. Please teach me Your ways. . .

MY PEOPLE

On the day you were born, you opened your eyes for the first time, and you saw your mom. You might have seen your dad smiling down at you, and doctors and nurses. You didn't know who any of these people were, but they were the first humans God introduced you to. From that day on, more people entered your life—sisters, brothers, grandparents, aunts, uncles, cousins, friends, teachers. . .your list of people got longer and longer. You are still adding people to that list.

Each person God brings into your life has a purpose. Some will bring you love, joy, and learning. Others won't set such good examples. Their purpose is to help you understand the difference between right and wrong.

Think about the older people in your life: your parents, grandparents, uncles, and aunts. What do you think is their purpose? Maybe Grandma taught you a special skill, like baking. Grandpa might have shared stories about when he was little that helped you understand what life was like long ago. If your aunt likes crafting, maybe you learned from her how to make things. If your uncle plays sports and works out, he might encourage you to keep your body healthy and strong. Your parents' purpose is to help you grow up and teach you about life.

Now think about the people you know who are around your age. What is their purpose? Your sisters and brothers help you learn about sharing and to work out differences when you don't get along. You and your friends share many of the same interests. Your friends' purpose is to bring fun into your life. If you choose friends who love God, then together you can help one another grow closer to Him and even serve Him as helpers in your community.

And what about your teachers? A teacher's purpose is to introduce you to all kinds of things you didn't know about. There's a big, beautiful world to discover, and teachers are your guide.

The best teacher of all is God's Son, Jesus. His purpose is to lead you. If you listen to His instructions and follow His ways, Jesus will lead you to the special purpose God has planned for you.

Jesus said to them, "Follow Me."
MATTHEW 4:19

Dear God, help me to know Jesus. . .

WHO IS JESUS?

When God created humans, He gave them rules. God wanted everyone He created to live with Him in heaven after they died. But to be with God, their hidden hearts had to be perfectly clean of sin—and sin is all the things God tells you are wrong. Sin has no place in heaven. God knew if people followed His rules, their hidden hearts would be clean of everything bad.

People kept breaking the rules. Still, God wanted their hearts perfectly clean and good enough for heaven. So, God made a plan. He sent His Son, Jesus, to earth to save people from sin.

Jesus arrived as a baby born to Mary, the special mom God chose for Him. When Jesus grew up, He became the world's greatest teacher. He reminded people to live right and follow God's rules. Jesus is a part of God, so He has the same godly powers. He did amazing miracles. Only God's Son could do such things! Many people trusted and followed Jesus. But some hated Him. They didn't believe He was God's Son.

Those who hated Jesus arrested Him. They nailed Him to a wooden cross to die. Then God did what He planned all along. He allowed Jesus to take into His heart all the sinful things people would ever do. Jesus took the punishment for the sins everyone would ever commit. God promised that anyone who trusted in Jesus and asked for forgiveness for their sins would be forgiven. Their hidden hearts would be made perfectly clean and ready for heaven when they died.

Jesus is the only way to heaven. He died taking the punishment for all the bad things we'll do. But there's more—Jesus came back from being dead. His body rose from the grave and people saw Him. Jesus promised us life forever in heaven with Him. Then, He left earth and went back to be with God.

Jesus' Spirit is with us today. He is a part of God with all of God's power. He is always with you, so You can talk with Him in prayer. Jesus is your very best friend.

*"For God so loved the world that He gave His only
Son. Whoever puts his trust in God's Son will not
be lost but will have life that lasts forever."*
JOHN 3:16

Dear Jesus, thank You for being my way to heaven. . .

GOD'S PLAN FOR ME

God has a special plan for you. He has a plan for every human He has ever put on earth. Each person's plan is special and designed just for him or her.

Some parts of God's plan for you are the same as His plan for everyone. God wants you to obey His rules. He wants you to know Him and to trust in His power to control everything in the universe. God wants you to believe in His Son, Jesus, and to trust that Jesus took the punishment for your sins. He wants you to love Jesus, learn about Him, and do your best to be like Him.

Along with those common things, God has already planned your entire life. When He created you, He planned every minute of your every day. You can't know the plan. But you will see parts of it unfold as you grow older. One day when you are very old, you might look back and see how God planned for you to serve Him and help others.

When God made you, He gave you special gifts—skills and talents—things you are good at. If you choose to trust God and follow Him, He will show you how to use His gifts to do good things. As you grow, God will help your skills and talents grow along with you. He will guide you into situations where you can use them to make the world a better place.

Think about those things you are good at. What are your favorite subjects in school? Do you like to sing, dance, or create things? Are you super-good at noticing what people need and being a helper? Are you good at comforting people when they are sad or caring for them when they are sick? Do you like traveling and discovering new things? Are you great at teaching your younger sister or brother to do something new? What are you good at? Ask God to help you recognize your special gifts and to use them to serve Him and others.

✳

"For I know the plans I have for you," says the Lord, "plans for well-being and not for trouble, to give you a future and a hope."
JEREMIAH 29:11

Dear God, make me aware of my special talents and skills. Guide me to use them to serve You. . .

DAY 5
WHAT'S YOUR STYLE?

Are you a fashionista? Nail polish, new hairstyles, bracelets and beads, sandals, hats, tees, totes, jeans, maybe a cute sundress or two. . . You want to look your best, and there are so many styles to choose from.

What is your favorite style? Do you feel most at home in shorts, a T-shirt, a bucket hat, and flip-flops? Maybe you're a girly girl who loves dresses, pretty hair clips, cool sunglasses, and floppy straw hats. Or maybe you have a one-of-a-kind style. You dare to put together wild colors and patterns, and you have a huge collection of socks with crazy patterns— unicorns, rainbows, stars, stripes. . . You make your own bracelets and necklaces to match your favorite outfits.

Look around you. Everyone has a style, a way of dressing that is most comfortable for them. It's important to keep your body looking good; and however you decide to dress, it's important to keep your body healthy, neat, and clean.

There's another kind of style. The Bible says this kind of style is way more important than looking beautiful on the outside. This kind of style comes from your hidden heart. When you fill up your heart with a gentle, quiet spirit that cares about others, your inner beauty will shine through to the outside for all to see. People will notice your caring personality. Add to your style friendliness, honesty, kindness, trustworthiness, patience, joy, and love. Can you think of more traits to tuck inside your hidden heart?

Be the kind of girl who, when she enters the room, people notice because of her personality. Let your inner beauty shine. Connect with others not because you look similar on the outside but because you connect with your hearts. That's the kind of connection God wants you to make. The Bible says your heart's beauty is beauty that lasts. It is of great worth that no amount of money can buy.

✱

Your beauty should come from the inside. It should come from the heart. This is the kind that lasts. Your beauty should be a gentle and quiet spirit. In God's sight this is of great worth and no amount of money can buy it.
1 PETER 3:4

Dear God, fill up my heart with the kind of beauty that shines from the inside out. . .

BEAUTiFUL QUEEN ESTHER

Esther was a beautiful Jewish girl who lived many centuries ago in Persia. (Today, it's Iran.) Her parents had died, and she was raised by her older cousin, a man named Mordecai.

When the Persian king, Ahasuerus, was looking for a beautiful woman to marry, he ordered his men to search the kingdom. They found Esther. Mordecai knew the king wasn't Jewish, and he told Esther not to tell them she was a Jew. He worried if the king found out, he wouldn't take her as his queen. So, Esther kept her nationality a secret.

After Esther married King Ahasuerus, Mordecai spent every day hanging around outside the castle keeping watch over her. Often, Haman, the king's special representative, walked by and commanded those outside the castle to bow to him. But Mordecai refused. This made Haman angry, so he tricked the king into sentencing to death all the Jews in his kingdom. When Mordecai found out, he told Esther.

Esther knew she had to tell the king! She had to save her people. But no one was allowed to visit the king without an invitation—not even his wife. If Esther disobeyed, she could be put to death. She needed to decide. If she waited for the king's invitation, her people, the Jews, would die. If she were courageous and went uninvited to the king, she might be able to save them.

Esther was beautiful on the outside, but she also had a beautiful heart. She wanted to do what she knew was right.

So, she chose courage. She confessed to the king that she was a Jew. She told him of Haman's evil plot to kill her people. Then King Ahasuerus punished Haman. He stopped the Jews from being killed.

Some decisions are hard. What would you have done? Would you have kept quiet about the evil plan, or would you have said something to save your family and friends?

God put Esther in just the right place at just the right time to save her people's lives.

❋

"For if you keep quiet at this time, help will come to the Jews from another place. But you and your father's house will be destroyed. Who knows if you have not become queen for such a time as this?"
ESTHER 4:14

Dear God, help me with hard decisions.
I want to do what's right. . .

BUTTERFLIES

Butterflies in your stomach. You know the feeling. It's the night before the first day at a new school, and those butterflies are acting up. They're flitting around inside, making you feel anxious. It's not just the first day of school when they take flight. It's every time you face something new or unexpected. It's not a good feeling. You might want to make those butterflies settle by backing down and avoiding anything that makes them fly. But—think about it—if you did that, you would never try anything new. You could miss out on some cool new experiences. You might never meet the person who would become a best friend or, when you get older, the man you would marry. If you hid in your house for the rest of your life, you would forever avoid that butterfly feeling, but you would end up miserable and alone.

New experiences take courage. They require you to take one first, brave step into the unknown. Courage means silencing that little voice inside that says you aren't good enough, smart enough, pretty enough, strong enough. . .and instead listening to God's voice telling you, "I made you to be courageous and strong, and lovely, and good, and wise." Listening to God's voice speaking inside your heart and believing He will give you courage and strength are ways of settling those butterflies.

God says He is the one who goes with you. He's not just there when you call on Him for help. He is with you every second of every minute of every day. God will never leave you.

When you take that courageous first step toward something new, He is the one who leads you to the next step and the next, and before long, that scary new experience won't feel so scary anymore. Your heart will fill up with such courage and strength that nothing can get in your way.

Trust God. He loves you. He will give you some of His own power to face whatever comes your way.

"Be strong and have strength of heart. Do not be afraid or shake with fear because of them. For the Lord your God is the One Who goes with you. He will be faithful to you. He will not leave you alone."
DEUTERONOMY 31:6

Dear God, give me courage and strength. . .

DAY 8
DiFFiCULT PEOPLE

The Bible says God's army, the Israelites, were in a battle with the Philistines. The Philistines had a soldier twice as tall as any man in God's army. Goliath was big and scary. He was ready to fight. He had with him another soldier walking in front of him carrying his shield.

Goliath shouted to the Israelites, "Choose a man for yourselves, and let him come to me. If he is able to fight me and win, then we will be your servants. But if I fight him and win, then you must be our servants."

A young shepherd boy, David, arrived, bringing food for his brothers who were soldiers in God's army. When David heard Goliath making fun of God's army, he decided to do something. When no other soldier would stand up to the big soldier, David did. He took a stone and threw it. It hit Goliath on his forehead. The stone went into his forehead, and he fell on his face to the ground. So, David won the fight against the giant Philistine with one single stone.

People can be difficult to get along with sometimes. Just like Goliath, they can talk and act in ways that make others feel small. There are ways to stand up to Goliaths other than picking up a rock and firing it at their heads. If a Goliath tries to make you feel unimportant and small, first remember that God thinks you are the most important person in the world. You are His child. And no matter what anyone says, you are good and smart and capable. Sometimes, you can knock down a Goliath with stones of kindness, understanding, and caring. If kindness, understanding, and caring don't knock your Goliath down, it's okay to walk away.

Standing up to a Goliath takes courage. Everyone knows you are God's girl, courageous, brave, and strong. But there may be times when you need help with a Goliath. Telling your parents or another trusted adult that you need help is always a very courageous thing to do.

And there is one more thing you can do to knock a Goliath down. Pray for him (or her).

❃

"The Lord is my Helper. I am not afraid of anything man can do to me."
HEBREWS 13:6

Dear God, when I meet a "Goliath,"
show me what to do. . .

DAY 9
KiNDNESS

Can you think of a time when you needed some kindness and God sent a kind, caring person your way? She or he might have said just the right words to make you feel better. Or maybe you were having trouble understanding an assignment or getting something done, and a kind person came to your aid and provided the exact sort of help you needed. A little kindness can go a long way toward helping someone feel good about herself and what she does.

Think about this: Is there a quiet girl in your class who doesn't have many friends? How could you show her some kindness? Getting to know her is the first step. Talk with her, invite her to sit with you at lunch or play with you at recess, introduce her to some of your friends. That quiet girl might need only a little kindness to help her feel comfortable enough around others to make new friends.

When your mom comes home from work and you see a tired look on her face, would you react with kindness? Simple things like helping to get supper on the table and doing chores without being asked will show your mom that you understand how she feels. A loving hug and a few caring words would be another way to show her some kindness.

Kindness is keeping your eyes peeled for what others need and then trying your hardest to help. It's carrying packages, opening doors, giving compliments, picking up trash, cleaning a mess, making a card, sharing a treat, being patient, listening to problems, calling your grandparents. . . Think about all the little ways people show kindness toward each other every day.

When you fill your hidden heart with kindness, it's going to spill out for all to see. People will notice. Their trust in you will grow because they will see you as someone they can count on for help. When you show kindness toward others, you will be setting a good example for them. Your acts of kindness will inspire others and teach them to be kind.

What can you do today, right now, to show some kindness to someone?

If someone has the gift of showing kindness to others, he should be happy as he does it.
Romans 12:8

Dear God, please remind me to be kind. . .

DAY 10
PATIENCE

Waiting can be difficult. When there's something you want to happen, a task you want to accomplish, someplace you want to be, or someone you want to see, waiting can feel excruciating—that's a big word that means "really uncomfortable." Sometimes, waiting just one more minute can seem like forever. When you want something right away and you can't have it, impatience might lead you to feel anxious and even grumpy.

Everyone has certain personality traits they are born with. Some people are born with patience already tucked inside their hearts. But for most of us, patience is something we learn. It takes practice.

Imagine you want your dad to drive you to hang out at a friend's house, but your dad is busy working in the yard. He promises he will take you as soon as he can, but you want to go right now. How would you react? Would you be angry with your dad for not doing what you want when you want it? Being patient means trusting that your dad will do what he said: he will take you as soon as he can. In the meantime, you might offer to help him with the yardwork. The Bible says, "Two are better than one" (Ecclesiastes 4:9). The two of you working together could get you where you want to be sooner, and it will give you something to do while you wait.

Learning patience takes creative thinking. It means coming up with ideas of how you can make the waiting easier. Say you are trying to accomplish something, and you find yourself getting impatient because the project isn't done. Taking a short break can stop that impatient feeling and help you try again when you feel more refreshed. You could also check to see if feeling impatient comes from being selfish. We're all a little selfish sometimes. Learning patience comes from putting the needs of others before your own. It's being understanding and caring even when you don't feel like it.

The Bible says, "Be patient with everyone" (1 Thessalonians 5:14 NIV). Can you think of three things you can do today to help you become more patient?

✺

You should be kind to others and have no pride.
Be gentle and be willing to wait for others.
COLOSSIANS 3:12

Dear God, please guide me to become more patient. . .

WAITING FOR GOD

There is a Bible story about a man named Job. He loved God and always did his best to please Him. Job talked with God often, and he had great faith in God. He trusted that God would always do what He promised.

God had blessed Job with a wonderful life, but then terrible things began to happen. Some of Job's animals were stolen and others were killed. Job earned his living raising and selling animals, like some farmers do today. So, the loss of his animals made him a poor man. Then, Job's servants died and so did some of his family members. And if that weren't bad enough, Job began getting sores on his body. They covered him from head to toe. Job's friends criticized him. "You must have done something to displease God," they suggested. "It has to be your fault causing these things to happen."

Through it all, Job prayed. He had many conversations with God. He asked, "Why is this happening to me?" He was totally miserable, and God seemed far away. Job's prayers weren't being answered, and his friends even suggested he might be better off if he were dead. But Job refused to lose faith in God. He waited, believing that somehow, some way, God would turn things around.

What Job didn't know was God was watching it all, testing Job's faithfulness. God wanted to prove to Satan (the evil one who causes bad things to happen) that nothing would stop Job from loving God and trusting in Him.

After Job proved His faithfulness, God cleared up Job's sores. He gave him twice as many animals as he'd had, and Job became even wealthier than he'd been before. Job's family grew. He had seven sons and three daughters, and Job lived to be a much-loved and respected old man.

If something bad happened, would you still trust God to help you? Do you think you could have patience like Job's and wait for God to answer your prayers even if it took a very long time?

✳

But they who wait upon the Lord will get new strength. They will rise up with wings like eagles. They will run and not get tired. They will walk and not become weak.
ISAIAH 40:31

Dear God, I will wait patiently for You to answer my prayers. . .

DAY 12
TALKING WITH GOD

Prayer is simply talking with God. You don't have to be in church to pray or kneel beside your bed. You can talk with God anytime anywhere. God is with you all the time. You are His child, and He wants to hear from you. Although He already knows everything about you and all that's happening in your life, He still wants you to talk with Him and tell Him your thoughts. God is your best friend, and you can talk with Him just as you would a friend. You can trust God with your deepest secrets. Even if you had done something that displeased Him, even if you felt embarrassed, you could still come to God and be certain He wouldn't be angry with you. If you tell Him you are sorry, God will forgive you for anything!

A conversation is two people talking with each other. You won't hear God talking out loud, but you will hear Him in your thoughts. He speaks to you inside your heart. God's voice is more like a whisper. It's that little voice inside reminding you to do what is right and to avoid what's wrong. It's that small voice that says, "Don't worry. Don't be afraid. I will help you."

While it's true you can pray anytime and anywhere, it's important to set aside some quiet time when you can give God all your attention. Find a quiet place where you can go to pray. Make it your special place to meet with God every day. When you pray, don't just talk. Take time to listen. Sit quietly and wait. Try to clear your head of everything that's on your mind, then listen for God in your thoughts. God doesn't often use many words when He speaks, and sometimes He remains silent. That doesn't mean He's not real, He's not listening, or He doesn't care. God does everything in His own time, and He will speak His words to you exactly when you need to hear them.

Praying leads you nearer to God. It's connecting your hidden heart with His. What would you like to tell God today?

But it is sure that God has heard. He has listened to the voice of my prayer.
PSALM 66:19

Dear God, teach me to hear You
and recognize Your voice. . .

GOD IS REAL

Take a deep breath. Let it out. Could you see the air entering and leaving your body? Jump up and down. Could you see gravity pulling you back to earth? Be quiet and listen. Can you see the sounds you hear?

Many things exist that you can't see. How about the Wi-Fi that connects your tablet to the world? Or electricity that makes lightbulbs light up? Can you see thoughts, feelings, heat, or cold? There is evidence these things exist, but you can't see them with your eyes.

It's the same with God. You can't see Him with your eyes, but you know He exists. God made everything in the universe. The Bible says God has existed forever. He has no beginning or end. He created the earth, the sun, moon, and stars. He made all the animals, plants, and people. He made the air you breathe, the water and food you need to live, and He made your body parts work together perfectly to keep you alive. You can "see" God in the miracles He did in the Bible. He made the water in the Red Sea part so His people could walk on dry land from shore to shore. He made food rain down from the sky when His people were hungry. He saved the lives of men who were threatened by fire, hungry lions, and angry waves. God still does miracles today. We hear of people sensing danger and getting out of its way and the sick getting well even when doctors said they wouldn't.

God is real. This same God who created the universe, every-thing in it—and you!—wants to be your heavenly Father. He thinks of you as His child. Every day He cares for, loves, and protects you because you belong to Him. You cannot see God yet. When you get to heaven someday, you will. Faith means believing in what you cannot see. Having faith, you can trust that God exists. He is the one and only God, and He is real.

✻

We do not look at the things that can be seen. We look at the things that cannot be seen. The things that can be seen will come to an end. But the things that cannot be seen will last forever.
2 CORINTHIANS 4:18

Dear God, I "see" You all around me
in everything You've made. . .

EVERYWHERE ALL THE TIME

Who do you believe is the smartest person on earth? Since the beginning of time, people have put their faith in the knowledge of kings, queens, presidents, scientists, doctors, inventors, astronomers, mathematicians. The Bible tells of a very wise man named Solomon. God gave him all kinds of wisdom about life. The book of Proverbs in the Bible holds a collection of Solomon's wise sayings. Still, as smart as Solomon and other men and women were and are today, none comes close to the mind of God. He knows everything that has happened in the past, everything that is going on right now, and what will happen in the future.

The Bible tells us God is everywhere all the time, and He knows everything. It says God knows how many stars are in the sky. He has given each star a name. He knows the number of hairs on your head (even how many come out on your comb or brush). God knows when you cry. The Bible says He collects your tears in His bottle. If even one bird falls out of the sky, God knows. God has the amazing, unimaginable superpower of knowing everything that is going on with everyone on earth this very minute. And add to that He knows what will happen to each of us in the next minute and the next throughout our entire lives.

Time and space don't exist for God as they do for us. We can't begin to understand how He can be everywhere all at once or know everything all the time. It's one of the mysteries about Him that we believe by faith.

A very wise king in the Bible, King David, said to God: "Is there any place I can go to avoid your Spirit? to be out of your sight? If I climb to the sky, you're there! If I go underground, you're there! If I flew on morning's wings to the far western horizon, You'd find me in a minute—you're already there waiting!" (Psalm 139:7–12 MSG).

How do you feel about God being everywhere all the time? Are you glad He's always with you?

He knows the number of the stars.
He gives names to all of them.
Psalm 147:4

Dear God, You are everywhere all the time. You see me and know me. . .

CHOOSING TO OBEY

Not only is God everywhere all the time, but He has power over everything all the time. God controls everything on earth, in the universe, and in heaven. How God decides to use His power is another of the mysteries about Him. We wonder: if God has power over everyone and everything, why do bad things happen?

When God creates people, He doesn't make them like robots. He doesn't write a code and program people to do His will. Instead, God allows people to make choices. He sets rules He wants them to follow, rules that will lead people toward doing what's right, but God leaves it up to people to decide whether they will obey His rules.

Adam and Eve were the first people God made. He put them in a beautiful perfect garden with everything they needed to live perfect lives. He gave them only one rule—not to eat fruit from one special tree in the garden. It was the Tree of Knowledge of Good and Evil. Adam and Eve didn't know evil existed, but if they ate the fruit, then they would know. God allowed the devil, Satan, to test Adam and Eve to see if they would obey His rule. Instead of obeying, Adam and Eve followed Satan's suggestion to eat the fruit. Their choice allowed evil to enter the garden and the world. Could God have stopped it? Yes. God can do anything. But He let Adam and Eve choose.

God always allows us to choose. Think about this: when you make a choice to disobey your parents' rules, there are consequences. The same is true for everyone, kids and grown-ups alike. When we disobey the rules, there are consequences. Sometimes that means bad things come from the choices we make.

The good news is when people make wrong choices, God has absolute power to make something good come from them. It might be a lesson learned or some sort of unexpected help. You might not notice something good come from a bad choice, but God makes us this promise: it is part of His perfect plan that all things work for good for those who love Him (Romans 8:28).

Can you think of something good that came from a bad choice?

"For God can do all things."
LUKE 1:37

Dear God, please help me obey Your rules. . .

SERVING GOD

Throughout history, kings have sent their servants into the world to carry out the king's business. In Bible stories, kings' servants were often messengers. They traveled around kingdoms telling the kings' subjects about laws the kings set and what they expected their people to do. Kings wanted their servants to work hard for them and serve willingly and even joyfully.

God is King of everything. He makes rules that He wants us to obey. God has appointed those who love Him to be His servants and carry His messages to the world.

Maybe you've heard your pastor or youth group leader speak about "serving the Lord." Pastors serve God by teaching about Him and reminding people how God wants them to live. Missionaries serve God by setting up churches in faraway countries. They teach people about Jesus and explain that He is the way to heaven. Teaching others who God is, what He expects, and why His Son, Jesus, came to earth is one very important way to serve God. But there are many other ways to serve Him.

Think of yourself as God's representative on earth. It's your job to set a good example for others. You serve God by following His rules, getting along well with others, having a positive attitude, being kind and caring, sharing your things, being a helper, working hard, doing your best. . . All these things set a good example for others to follow. You serve God when you willingly do what pleases Him. If you share with your family and friends what you know about God and Jesus, you are an even better servant because you are helping to carry God's messages to the world.

How can you serve God today? Start at home by obeying the rules, helping around the house, and having a good attitude. At school, work hard, do your best, be welcoming to others, and try to get along with everyone. Look around your neighborhood and community. Think of ways you can help there, then put your ideas into action.

When you pray today, ask God to make you His servant and to use you to carry His good news to the world.

❋

Be glad as you serve the Lord. Come before Him with songs of joy.
PSALM 100:2

Dear God, make me Your servant.
What can I do for You today? . . .

RELATIONSHIPS

Jesus' followers called Him "Rabbi." It's a word that means "teacher." Jesus was the best teacher ever. He had all God's power, so the words He spoke when He lived on earth were God's words. Jesus had the perfect answer for any question, and He always chose just the right words to lead people to think about God and what God expected from them.

About relationships, Jesus offered one simple but perfect rule. He said, "Do for other people whatever you would like to have them do for you" (Matthew 7:12). Think about your relationship with your parents, siblings, friends, teachers, classmates, and even people you don't know. Do you always do for others what you would like them to do for you?

If you expect your mom and dad to help when you need it, then shouldn't you help your parents when they need help? If you expect your sister to lend you her necklace, then shouldn't you allow her to borrow your sweater when she asks?

Jesus wants us to be considerate. That means imagining ourselves in the other person's situation and doing for him or her what we would want in the same situation. If you felt sad and lonely, what would you want someone to do for you? If you forgot to bring your packed lunch to school, what would you want someone to do for you? When you put yourself in another person's situation and act in a caring, helpful way, you will learn to be considerate. Better yet, you are doing what

Jesus taught! You are learning to get along with others in the best possible way.

About doing for others, Jesus added this. He said, "I tell you, love your enemies. Help and give without expecting a return. You'll never—I promise—regret it. . . . Our Father is kind; you be kind" (Luke 6:35–36 MSG). Doing for others isn't easy when the one you are doing for doesn't seem to appreciate what you've done. But be considerate anyway. Jesus sees you following His rule. You are pleasing Him by being kind. And pleasing Jesus is the most important thing of all.

Were you kind and considerate today?

"Do for other people whatever you would like to have them do for you."
MATTHEW 7:12

Dear God, remind me to act in ways that are considerate and kind, expecting nothing in return. . .

WORDS

Try this activity: Listen closely when people talk. Think about their words. Listen to your family members talking at home or in the car. Listen to your teachers and classmates. Listen to people around you who you don't know. As you listen, ask yourself, "Would those words be pleasing to God?"

It is never pleasing to God when people use swear words, especially if those words use God's or Jesus' name. Angry words don't please God either. And when people use their words to argue and hurt each other, those words hurt God's ears. The Bible says God hates it when He hears people lie. It also displeases God when people gossip. That means having conversations with friends about someone's personal business or sharing a rumor—information about someone you heard from someone else. Proud speech, which is bragging about how great you are, isn't pleasing to God either.

That's a lot to think about, isn't it?

The words you speak have a ton of power. You can choose words that knock people down and make them feel awful about themselves, or you can choose words to build people up so they feel good about themselves. You can choose words that make people feel afraid, or hurt them so badly they cry, or you can choose words that help people feel accepted, happy, and safe. Solomon (that wise man whose thoughts make up the book of Proverbs) had much to say about words. He warned that words can be like a sharp sword and hurt people (Proverbs 12:18). He said words can destroy relationships (Proverbs 11:9). Solomon also said, "Kind words heal and help" (Proverbs 15:4 MSG).

After you've listened to what others say and have thought about their words, spend time listening to your own words. Do you swear or use God's or Jesus' names in ways that are disrespectful? Do you choose words that build people up instead of knocking them down? Do you always tell the truth?

God hears every word you say, so be wise when choosing your words.

✱

Let the words of my mouth and the thoughts
of my heart be pleasing in Your eyes, O Lord,
my Rock and the One Who saves me.
PSALM 19:14

Dear God, I will choose my words carefully.
I want them to be like music to Your ears. . .

HOLY SPIRIT

God is sometimes called "Heavenly Father." God is the one who made us. He loves us with a perfect kind of fatherly love. As great as your dad might be, God the Father is even better. That's because God is perfect in every way. God is absolutely perfect. Everything He says is perfectly true. No human is perfect, not even your dad. (Still, your dad might be so awesome that you think he is perfect, and you hope to grow up to be just like him.)

The Bible warns us about Satan, the devil. He is called "the father of lies." Satan has a way of getting into your thoughts. His voice says, "You're not pretty." "You're not good enough." "Nobody loves you." That's not true! God says you are beautiful and loved just as you are. Satan's words will try to confuse you when you need to choose between doing what's right or wrong. It's his voice that says, "Come on. Do it. It'll be fun. Just watch out so you won't get caught."

It's important that you learn the difference between God's words and Satan's words.

You already know that Jesus is God's Son. He is a part of who God is, and He has been with God forever. There is a third part of God that has been with Him forever. It is the Holy Spirit. He helps us hear God's voice inside our hidden hearts and leads us to do what's right. The Holy Spirit's voice speaks inside your heart, "You look nice today." He says, "God loves you." If you are about to make a wrong choice, the

42

Holy Spirit will tell you, "Wait. Stop. Are you sure you want to do that?"

You can ask God's Holy Spirit to help you recognize Satan's words and shut them out of your heart. No one wants to listen to a liar, so when you recognize the father of lies speaking inside your heart, tell him, "Go away!"

✳

"The devil has nothing to do with the truth. There is no truth in him. It is expected of the devil to lie, for he is a liar and the father of lies."
JOHN 8:44

Dear God, teach me to recognize Satan's words and to shut them out of my heart. . .

TRUTHFULNESS

How honest are you? Tell the truth: Have you ever in your life told a lie? Maybe just a tiny one? Lying is never pleasing to God. He doesn't see a difference between a little lie and a big one. If you are honest with God and say, "Dear Heavenly Father, I told a lie, and I'm sorry," you can be sure God will forgive you. He will always forgive you when you tell the truth and are sorry.

Can you think of a few reasons why people lie? Sometimes, they lie to avoid being punished or to keep someone else from being punished. People might lie because they feel embarrassed. For example, if you were to give a wrong answer to a question your teacher asked, to avoid your embarrassment you might reply, "I knew that! I just forgot." That would be a lie. People sometimes lie to make themselves look important or to be accepted by those who have opinions different from theirs. A few people tell so many lies that it becomes a habit. When that happens, they get really good at ignoring the Holy Spirit's voice inside their hearts when He says, "Stop. Don't lie!"

God expects you to tell the truth. The only time He might be accepting of a lie is if you are in danger and a lie will help to save your life or keep you safe. Hopefully, that will never happen to you. In your everyday life, it is important to always tell the truth.

When you tell the truth, others will notice. They will know they can trust you. If you have strong feelings about what is right and wrong, and if you stand up for what you believe in, people will respect you. You will show them that you are a leader instead of someone who gives in to peer pressure. (That means following what others do even if you know it's wrong.) When you tell the truth, you set a good example. God hears every word you speak. When you are honest, God is pleased. You might even hear Him say inside your heart, "That's my girl!"

"Speak the truth to one another."
ZECHARIAH 8:16

Dear God, if a lie should ever slip from my mouth, please forgive me. I will do my best to always tell the truth. . .

PEER PRESSURE

You love hanging out with your friends. Most girls you know do their best to obey the rules, but there are a few who don't. They want to try new things, even if their parents say, "No."

Imagine you are at a sleepover at a friend's house. Her mom says there are certain videos you can watch together, but she doesn't want you watching TV. You can stay up all night talking if you want. You can play games and enjoy as many snacks as you want. But no television. Your friend's mom trusts all of you to obey her rules. At bedtime, she checks on you girls and says, "I'm going upstairs to bed now. Behave yourselves, and let me know if you need anything." After she's been gone a while, your friend, the one whose house it is, puts on a television show you know your parents wouldn't approve of. She turns the volume way down so her mom won't hear. This is one of those situations where you have to choose. Would you go along with the others and watch, or would you find something else to do?

It's a tough decision when your friends want you to follow along with something that's against the rules. You want them to like you. You don't want to spoil the fun. But you know right from wrong. You know God wants you to choose what is right. You have two voices inside your hidden heart telling you what to do. The Holy Spirit says, "Follow the rules." The father of lies says, "Go ahead. Do it. Have fun!"

When you face peer pressure—it means your friends leading you toward what you know is wrong—do what you know is right. Sometimes, that's finding something else to do, and sometimes it means walking away from a situation altogether. One thing you can do is think in advance how you will handle it if someone wants you to do something you know is wrong. Talk with your parents about this, or even your older siblings. Ask them to give you some advice. Then trust God to help you do the right thing.

❋

"Do not follow many people in doing wrong."
EXODUS 23:2

Dear God, if I feel led toward doing something wrong, please lead me back to doing what is right. . .

SHADRACH, MESHACH, AND ABEDNEGO

The Bible tells us about three young men, Shadrach, Meshach, and Abednego. They were special servants to a king named Nebuchadnezzar.

The king did not believe there was only one God, and he didn't follow God's rules. One of God's rules said: "Do not make for yourselves a god to look like anything that is in heaven above or on the earth below or in the waters under the earth" (Exodus 20:4). God wants everyone to worship only Him, not a statue, an animal, or anything else. But the king didn't care. He had a huge, gold statue built, and he ordered everyone to bow to it. He declared that anyone who didn't obey and bow to this false god would be thrown into a fiery furnace.

Most in the kingdom did what the king said, they bowed. But Shadrach, Meshach, and Abednego refused. They chose to follow God's rule instead, even if it cost them their lives. That's how much they loved God and trusted that He would help them.

The king did what he promised. He had the men thrown into the furnace. But then something amazing happened. As the king watched, he saw four men in the fire instead of three. "Look!" said the king. "I see four men loose and walking about in the fire without being hurt! And the fourth one looks like . . . the Son of God!" (Daniel 3:25). He called Shadrach, Meshach, and Abednego to come out, and they did. None of them were burned. The king knew that their God had saved them. Then King Nebuchadnezzar commanded his people never to say anything against the one and only God.

If you had been there, would you have joined in with all the others and bowed to the statue of a false god, or would you have done what God wanted and worshipped only Him?

Shadrach, Meshach, and Abednego are good examples of having the courage to follow God's rules instead of giving in to peer pressure. When you stand up for what you believe is right, God will stand up with you. He will always guide and protect you when you follow His rules.

✳

If sinners try to lead you into sin, do not go with them.
PROVERBS 1:10

Dear God, I want to be courageous like Shadrach, Meshach, and Abednego, and follow Your rules. . .

THE TEN COMMANDMENTS

Long ago, God gave us ten special rules to follow. They are called the "Ten Commandments." Maybe you know what they are:

1. Do not have any other gods besides Me.

2. Do not worship any false gods.

3. Do not use My name in a disrespectful way.

4. Remember the Sabbath Day and keep it holy. (This means set aside Sunday as a special day to honor God.)

5. Respect your father and your mother.

6. Do not kill.

7. Be faithful to your husband or wife.

8. Do not steal.

9. Do not tell lies about others.

10. Do not want anything that belongs to someone else.

God gave us these and many other rules He wants us to obey. You will discover them as you read your Bible. God knows humans can't be perfect and follow all His rules all the time, but still, He expects us to try. When you practice following God's rules, you are learning to live the way God wants you to live. Memorize the Ten Commandments and think about them. How many of them have you obeyed?

Obey the Word of God.
JAMES 1:22

Dear God, I will memorize the Ten Commandments
and do my best to obey them. . .

51

FALSE GODS

In the days when the Bible was written, many people were worshipping false gods. These were imagined gods with names like Baal and Dagon. People made statues of their gods and worshipped them. While Moses, the leader of God's people, the Israelites, was high on a mountaintop getting the Ten Commandments from God, the Israelites made a statue of a golden calf. They had become tired of waiting for God, so they made their own god and bowed to it. This made God very angry.

Throughout history, people have believed in and even worshipped imaginary gods and goddesses. Mother Earth is an example. Some people praise and worship her. There is no Mother Earth—just God the Creator of Earth. Some people praise and worship the sun, moon, and stars. Others say certain kinds of animals are holy. All of this is very displeasing to God.

What is a false god? It is anything we make more important than God. Think about this: If God asked you to choose between spending time at the best theme park on earth or spending time with Him, which would you choose? If He asked you to choose between reading a chapter in a book you love or reading a chapter in the Bible, what would you do? God wants to be more important in your life than anyone or anything else. He wants you to focus your thoughts on Him all day long, to talk with Him all day, and to listen for His words in your heart. When you don't make God most important, then other things creep in and want most of your attention.

Begin each morning talking with God. Make it the first thing you do. Think of God as you go about your day. Get in the habit of saying little prayers to Him asking Him to help you and guide you. Praise Him for all the little blessings you see. Then end each day talking with God just before you go to sleep. When you keep God always on your mind, you will be less likely to make something or someone so important that it becomes a false god in your life.

My children, keep yourselves from false gods.
1 JOHN 5:21

Dear God, please remind me to put You
first in everything all the time. . .

PRAISE

Have you attended a graduation ceremony? When a graduate receives a diploma, people clap and cheer. Afterward, the graduate's friends and family say things like "Well done! Good job! I'm so proud of you!" They praise the accomplishments and give the graduate all the honor she or he deserves.

God wants to be honored and praised too. After all, He is the one responsible for every good thing on earth. God gives people the brains, skills, and talent to do great things—like become a graduate and earn a diploma.

David (Remember him? He was the young shepherd boy who fought the big soldier, Goliath.) grew up to be a king. David was a songwriter too. He wrote lyrics that praised and honored God. David's songs are called "psalms." The Old Testament book named Psalms is a collection of praise songs and poems, and David wrote many of them.

David believed that everything God ever made should praise Him. He wrote: "Praise Him, all His angels! Praise Him, all His army! Praise Him, sun and moon! Praise Him, all you shining stars! Praise Him, you highest heavens, and you waters above the heavens!" (Psalm 148:2–4). Can you imagine what it might sound like if everything God ever made had a voice and if they all together sang praises to Him? It would be the most beautiful music ever, a special kind of sound fit for heaven, a song sung for the King of all kings as He sits on His heavenly throne.

God is the only God. He is greater than anyone or anything, and God should be praised for all the amazing and wonderful things He does.

What are some ways you can praise God? You can sing a song to honor Him or play a praise song on a musical instrument. You might make up a poem about God's goodness or create a dance to perform in His honor. Most often, though, praise comes during your quiet time with Him. When you pray, praise God. Tell Him you recognize all the amazing and wonderful things He does, and then thank Him.

"All the earth will. . .sing praises to You.
They will sing praises to Your name."
PSALM 66:4

Dear God, You are so great and worthy of praise.
I honor You for what You have done. . .

55

WORSHIP

Imagine you are at a friend's birthday party. It's a spa theme, and everyone is making themselves look pretty, getting their nails done, maybe even experimenting with face masks and makeup. One of the girls says, "I *adore* this sparkly, purple nail polish!" Her words make you understand that she really, *really* loves that polish. She thinks that polish is better than any of the others. And when she looks at that sparkly, purple polish glistening on her nails, her heart fills up with—*Wow!*

When you adore something, it means you have a very strong feeling of loving it. A similar word is *worship*. Worship is how we express our adoration for God when our hearts fill up with love for Him.

We worship God for His greatness. Who else is perfect all the time? Who else can be everywhere all the time and all-knowing all the time? We worship God for His creations, the sun, moon, stars, mountains, oceans, forests, animals, and people. When we think about who God is and what He does, our hearts fill up with *Wow!* We worship Him because He loves us. Everything God does is for us. His love for us fills our hearts with so much love for Him, we can only say, "Wow!" We feel amazed that this God who is so perfect, powerful, and great loves us. Worship is our expression of honoring God because of His greatness and His love. It is saying, "Wow, God! I think You are better than anything and everything else."

When people worship, they sometimes raise their hands up toward God and heaven. It is a way of showing God they want their hearts connected with His Spirit. Kneeling is another form of worship. It is bowing to God to show Him respect.

Can you name a few great things God has made or has done? How do you know God loves you? When you say your prayers today, worship God. Let your heart fill up with love and respect for Him. Kneel or raise your hands and say, "Wow, God, I adore You!"

✻

"God is Spirit. Those who worship Him must worship Him in spirit and in truth."
JOHN 4:24

Dear Heavenly Father, I worship You for Your greatness. I worship You because You love me. Father, I adore You. . .

A PERFECT BLEND

The Bible talks about the Israelites' long journey through the desert as they traveled to the land God had promised them. Moses, their leader, pitched a tent he used as a "meeting tent," a place where He could spend time alone with God and pray. God later commanded Moses to have the Israelites build a bigger and better meeting tent, a "tabernacle" where they could come to worship Him. You might think of it as the first church. God provided very specific instructions about how the tabernacle should be built.

When God creates people, He makes each with special skills and talents—things they are good at. It was no accident that, among the Israelites, God had brought together everyone with all the special skills and talents needed to build the meeting tent.

Some created the tent's covering. Others made the wood pieces, hooks, and pillars. Craftsmen created a special box to hold the stone tablets on which God had engraved His Ten Commandments. They made long pieces of wood to help carry the box from place to place as they traveled. A curtain, maybe made by the women, was created to hang in front of the special box. The workers made lampstands and lamps they could fill with oil to burn for light. They built an altar. All the able women made cloth. They brought into the meeting tent blue, purple, and red cloth and fine linen they had made.

Everyone worked hard for six days, and on the seventh day, they rested and honored God.

Can you think of an example of people today blending their skills and talents to create something good, something that would please God? It doesn't have to be something you build. Think about a choir. God brings together people with different voices that blend just right to make music. He brings great thinkers together to create rules and laws. God brings people with unique skills together to make daring rescues and to help cure people who are sick. God has a special way of bringing just the right people together at just the right times to get things done.

✻

"Let every able workman among you come and make all that the Lord has told us to make."
Exodus 35:10

Dear God, thank You for bringing us together to accomplish Your work here on earth. . .

DIFFERENCES

God created humans to be one of a kind. We are special and unique. God made us different from one another. When we think about our differences in positive ways, we can learn from each other. We learn not only to get along better but also to blend our differences to help one another and do great things.

Maybe you have a classmate whose family came from a country far away. That friend might be struggling to learn the language and fit in. You could help them learn. As you teach your friend new words and your culture—the common things people do in your city or town—you can also learn about theirs. The two of you might get to know each other so well that you could use your experience getting to know each other and learning from your differences to help welcome other new kids into your school.

Everyone is different. Some are born with physical limitations. At school, you could meet classmates with special needs. In most ways, they are just like you—they want to be friends, they want to be accepted, included, and have fun. Don't allow differences to get in the way of forming new friendships. You can talk with each other about the things you both like to do and discover which of those things you could do together. What could you learn about your friend that will help you understand his or her special need? Maybe your friend needs to be quiet sometimes, or maybe you need to learn patience if it takes a little longer to do things together. You can learn from your special needs friends how to be encouraging, helpful, understanding, and kind. They might learn from you that they can do things they only dreamed of doing.

Differences come in all colors, shapes, and sizes. You can find them all around you in people, places, and things.

Celebrate the differences. Notice how they blend together in good ways. See if you and your friends can combine your differences to help others and make the world a better place.

❋

If someone has the gift of helping others, then he should help. If someone has the gift of teaching, he should teach.
ROMANS 12:7

Dear God, help me to see differences in a positive way and how to blend them together to do something good. . .

FRIENDS

Think about your closest friends. God has a way of bringing people together exactly when they need each other. Some of your friendships might have started as play dates when you were very young. Others happened because you spent tons of time together in school as classmates. You likely have friends outside of school too, friends who attend your church or share your common interests like music, art, theater, or dance.

Friends are important. Not only do your closest friends hang out with you and do fun things, but their thoughts are a lot like yours. They know what it feels like to be a kid in a grown-up world. They understand better than an adult when you feel angry with the clouds when it rains on your birthday party or when you feel sad that the new boy in class made fun of your red hair. Your closest friends "get you." They understand you and stand up for you, no matter what.

God puts people all around you who might become your friends. If you are friendly and welcoming toward others, you will soon have a whole army of friends. Some might be in your life for just a short while, and others might be with you for a lifetime. Each friend will have a purpose in your life. Maybe it's just to share some fun and enjoy each other's company, or maybe it's to help you learn, gain confidence, or get through a difficult time.

What kind of friend are you? You will be the best kind of friend if you try to be like Jesus and act in ways that please God.

Today's Bible verse says, "There is a friend who stays nearer than a brother." That friend is Jesus. As you learn about Him, you will discover that He had many friends. People wanted to be around Him. They wanted to be like Him because He was a willing helper and a good role model.

Ask Jesus to help you make friends and also to be a good friend. Then trust Him to guide you.

A man who has friends must be a friend, but there is a friend who stays nearer than a brother.
PROVERBS 18:24

Dear Jesus, lead me to the friends You want me to have. Help me to be a good friend. . .

RUTH AND NAOMi

The book of Ruth tells the story of a great friendship between two women. One of them, Ruth, was a young married woman. The other, Naomi, was Ruth's mother-in-law, Ruth's husband's mother.

A sad thing happened. Both Ruth's and Naomi's husbands died. Ruth had family members who lived in another city. Naomi had no one. But Naomi did a very unselfish thing. She told Ruth to go home to be with her family. *I will be okay all alone*, Naomi thought. But then Ruth did something equally unselfish. She refused to leave Naomi. Ruth said, "Do not beg me to leave you or turn away from following you. I will go where you go. I will live where you live. Your people will be my people. And your God will be my God" (Ruth 1:16). What a loyal friend Ruth was! Instead of going home to her family, where she had friends her own age, she decided to stay with the older woman who had no one.

God saw what Ruth did. It was part of a secret plan He had for the two women. Ruth and Naomi traveled together to Bethlehem, where Naomi and her husband had once lived. When they arrived there, whom did they run into but a relative of Naomi's husband. Boaz was a rich and handsome man. Ruth and Boaz began dating. Their like for one another soon turned into love, and they got married. Ruth had a new husband! Before long, they had a baby boy. Naomi had a new family and a new home with Ruth, Boaz, and little Obed. But God's plan wasn't done yet. When Obed grew up, he had a son, and his son had a son, and that boy was David. He was the shepherd boy who struck down the giant soldier named Goliath, and later he became King David, Israel's greatest king.

Do you think you could be the kind of friend Ruth was to Naomi? Would you be willing to give up what you wanted to provide your friend with what she needs?

*Many will say they are loyal friends, but who
can find one who is truly reliable?*
PROVERBS 20:6 NLT

Dear God, help me become a loyal friend,
the kind of friend who gives up what
she wants for what others need. . .

DAY 31
LOVE EACH OTHER

When Jesus lived here on earth, He said, "I give you a new Law. You are to love each other. You must love each other as I have loved you" (John 13:34). A law is a command meant to be obeyed. Jesus commanded us to love each other, and He wants us to obey His law.

Wise King Solomon wrote, "A friend loves at all times" (Proverbs 17:17). What do you think that means? Do you always love your friends? How do they know you love them?

Love has different forms. There is the kissy, lovey kind of romantic love husbands and wives share. There is also a special kind of family love shared among parents and their children and brothers and sisters. There is another kind of love that shows we care for, respect, and understand the needs of others. That's the kind of love friends have for each other. They love one another because they care. A loving friend will always want what's best for you. She will care about you even if the two of you have an argument. She won't stop caring about you if you have a bad day and aren't as nice to her as she wants you to be. She will continue to care about and love you even if you mess up big time! A loving friend is always tuned in to what you need, and she will do her best to help you.

There is one more kind of love. It is the greatest of all. The Bible calls it *agape* (pronounced: uh-GAH-pay) love. It is God's perfect love for us. When Jesus said, "You must love each other as I have loved you," He was talking about agape love.

Jesus loves us perfectly, and He wants us to learn from Him what it means to love one another as dear and caring friends.

When you read and learn about Jesus, you will discover He always cared about the needs of others. He was a friend to all, even those who didn't have any friends. Jesus gave His friends wise advice. Most of all, Jesus wanted His friends to know and love God. Are you that kind of friend?

A friend loves at all times.
PROVERBS 17:17

Dear Jesus, teach me to be a loving
friend even when it's hard. . .

LOVE IS IMPORTANT

One of the greatest Jesus-followers in the Bible was a man named Paul. Paul didn't always love Jesus. After Jesus had died on the cross and come back to life, He told His disciples to go out into the world and tell everyone the good news—that God's Son had come and made a way for everyone to live in heaven. Paul had never met Jesus in person; still, for some reason, he hated anyone who loved and followed Him. The Bible doesn't say why Paul hated Christians, but we know he did.

Paul's big turnaround came one day when he was walking on a road and a bright light came down from heaven. It was so bright that Paul fell to the ground. A voice said, "Why are you working so hard against Me?" (Acts 9:4) It was Jesus! Paul had been blinded by the light, and he asked, "What do you want me to do, Lord?" (Acts 9:6) Jesus sent Paul to one of His followers, a man named Ananias. He healed Paul's eyes, and then Paul's hidden heart was filled with love for Jesus.

Paul joined other Jesus followers telling the good news to all who would listen. He suffered for it too. Paul was put in prison for talking about Jesus. But while He was there, He never stopped loving Jesus or caring about His Christian friends. He wrote letters to them from prison.

In one of His letters, Paul wrote about love. He said, "If I have the gift of speaking God's Word and if I understand all secrets, but do not have love, I am nothing. If I know all things and if I have the gift of faith so I can move mountains, but do not have love, I am nothing. If I give everything I have to feed poor people. . .but do not have love, it will not help me" (1 Corinthians 13:2–3). Paul understood the greatness of God's love. For him, God's love and sharing it was more important than anything.

Can you imagine a world without love? How do you think people would feel if no one loved or cared about them?

Your love means more than life to me, and I praise you.
PSALM 63:3 CEV

Dear God, Your love means everything to me. . .

TRUE LOVE

If you've ever tried training a puppy, you know it's not easy. You work at potty training, but there are messy accidents. You tell the puppy, "No!" But the puppy won't obey. When you're busy, the puppy begs for your attention. When the puppy disappoints you, you have a choice: you can give up on him, or you can patiently love and care for your puppy no matter what. Which would you choose?

Paul wrote about what true love looks like. He said, "Love does not give up" (1 Corinthians 13:4). Paul was talking about God's love. God's love is truly perfect. He never gives up on us. Even if we turn against God and walk away, He continues to love us, and He wants us to come back to Him. That's the kind of love God wants us to have for each other.

You love your brothers and sisters. Still, they can be irritating sometimes. Do you stop loving them when they irritate you? No. Your love for your siblings is greater than the irritation you feel when they annoy you. Their behavior might disturb you a dozen times a day, and still, you choose to love them.

True love—loving with God's kind of love—means being patient and forgiving. It means choosing to love someone even when they've hurt your feelings. It means loving even when you feel tired, frustrated, or angry. True love means not giving up on a friend who behaves badly. Sometimes, you might have to walk away from her bad behavior, but you can still choose to love and care about her and ask God to help her.

Paul understood true love, and he put it into action. Even in prison, he was patient, cooperative, and forgiving. Paul trusted in God's perfect love, and he did his best to be a good role model. He loved others with a godly, never-give-up kind of love.

Can you think of a time when it wasn't easy for you to love someone? God understands. When true love is hard, don't give up. Ask God to fill your heart with His perfect love. Ask Him to help you choose love over feelings of hurt and anger. And remember to pray for those who hurt you.

❋

Love does not give up.
1 CORINTHIANS 13:4

Dear God, help me to be patient
in love and not give up. . .

LOVE IS KIND

Paul remembered how it felt when God showed loving-kindness toward him even when he didn't deserve it. In a letter to his friend Timothy, Paul wrote: "Before He chose me, I talked bad about (Jesus). I made His followers suffer. I hurt them every way I could. But God had loving-kindness for me. I did not understand what I was doing for I was not a Christian then. . . . And yet God had loving-kindness for me. Jesus. . .used me to show how long He will wait for even the worst sinners" (1 Timothy 1:13, 16).

God saw the bad things Paul did, and yet He was patient with Paul. He kept loving him, no matter what. God was so kind that He forgave Paul for his wrongdoings. Then He opened Paul's eyes to the great plan He had for him—to follow Jesus and spread the good news. Years later, Paul hadn't forgotten God's loving-kindness. It led him to encourage others to love in a way that was patient and kind.

Jesus said, "Those who show loving-kindness are happy, because they will have loving-kindness shown to them" (Matthew 5:7). Has anyone been kind to you when you didn't deserve it? Did it make you feel happy? Happiness comes from being patient and kind. It comes from knowing you did the right thing. Even if you receive nothing in return, you can be sure God saw your kindness. When you know God is pleased with you, then you will have a happy heart.

Do you know someone who is grumpy, selfish, or uncooperative? Do something kind for that person today. It doesn't have to be anything big. Just do one little kind act. Let it be a secret between you and God. Then, even if the person doesn't notice, see if you feel happy for having done it. If you keep on doing kind things for those who are grumpy, selfish, and uncooperative, God just might use your kindness to open their eyes, like He did Paul's. Your acts of kindness might lead them to become Jesus followers, and that surely will give you a happy heart.

✳

"Those who show loving-kindness are happy, because they will have loving-kindness shown to them."
MATTHEW 5:7

Dear God, remind me to be loving and kind, even to those who don't deserve it. . .

JEALOUSY

Are you a good speller? Imagine you became so good at spelling that you entered competitions. You worked hard, and you became such an awesome speller that you qualified for the National Spelling Bee. You felt so proud! At the competition, you did very well in the preliminaries. You made it to the quarterfinals, and you were sure you were on your way to the semifinals and winning the medal and trophy cup. But then you were faced with an unfamiliar word. You guessed at the spelling, and you guessed wrong. After all your hard work and believing you would win, you were eliminated from the competition. How would you react?

You might react with jealousy—feeling unhappy that someone else got what you wanted. You might cry and say, "It's not fair!" If you were a jealous person, you might complain that you were given a harder word than the other competitors. You might even turn your hurt feelings toward the other competitors and blame them for taking from you what you felt you deserved. Jealousy isn't a good feeling. It keeps us from loving each other.

When Paul wrote about love, he said, "Love is not jealous" (1 Corinthians 13:4). Jealousy takes our eyes off our blessings. It can destroy relationships too. It is an unhappy, angry feeling that can grow inside our hidden hearts if we let it. So, it's important to recognize a jealous feeling right away and replace it with something else.

God understands that everyone feels jealous sometimes. We all want things. But God wants us to trust Him to give us what we need. When you feel jealous, ask God to help you replace your jealous feelings with love. Turn your thoughts toward all the good things God has given you. Practice being a good sport by congratulating those who win when you wish you had been the winner. Work hard at replacing jealousy with acts of loving-kindness. Be happy with yourself for your accomplishments, even if you don't win. And remember, in God's eyes, you are always a winner.

Can you think of a time you thought something wasn't fair? What did you do?

✳

Wherever you find jealousy and fighting, there will be trouble and every other kind of wrong-doing.
JAMES 3:16

Dear God, teach me to replace my jealous feelings with acts of loving-kindness. . .

PRIDE

Think about what you've accomplished in the past year. You've grown not only in size but also in what you know. You've earned responsibilities you didn't have when you were younger. You've put your skills and talents to work. Maybe you won a competition, or maybe you challenged yourself to do something physical, like participate in a charity walk or learn a new sport. You should be proud of what you've accomplished, and you should thank God—after all, He is the one who made it happen. God supplies you with all the qualities you need to get things done.

Being proud of what you've accomplished is a good thing, but it's not so good if pride becomes so big that it turns into a feeling of being better than others. When Paul wrote about love, he said, "Love does not put itself up as being important. Love has no pride" (1 Corinthians 13:4). He meant love can't exist in your hidden heart along with feelings of self-importance and being better than others.

Maybe you know a girl who is stuck up and snooty. Do you think she is someone people look up to as a role model? Do you believe others appreciate her *I'm-so-much-better-than-you* attitude? A stuck-up person can be so much about herself that she doesn't care about others. Her hidden heart is so filled with pride that all the loving-kindness gets pushed out. Can you imagine being so full of yourself that your heart doesn't have space for kindness and love? Pride can do that. It can push kindness right out of your heart.

When accepting an award or other honor, you might hear someone thank God. That person understands that God is responsible for our accomplishments. God deserves to be thanked first. Those who help us achieve our goals deserve thanks too. Giving thanks is a way of showing loving-kindness. After you have thanked God and others, then you can be pleased with yourself for what you have done.

Who can you thank today for helping you reach your goals? Remember to tell them, "Thank you."

✳

A man's pride will bring him down, but he whose
spirit is without pride will receive honor.
PROVERBS 29:23

Dear God, keep me from feeling too proud.
It is Your kindness and the kindness of others
that lead me to do great things. . .

JONAH

The book of Jonah in the Old Testament says God wanted Jonah to do something difficult. God wanted Jonah to go to a place called Nineveh, where the people didn't follow God's rules. He wanted Jonah to tell them God was watching and they needed to improve their behavior. God wanted everyone to turn from their unkind ways and follow Him. But Jonah didn't care. He thought of himself first and worried harm might come to him if he did what God said. So, Jonah ran away. He got on a big sailing ship and hid from God.

At sea, there was a great storm. The ship was in danger of sinking. The crew cried out to their false gods, but nothing changed. Then Jonah confessed that he was running from the one true God. The men blamed Jonah for making God angry and causing the storm. So, Jonah told them to throw him overboard. (Maybe he was afraid for his life if he stayed on the ship and thought he had a better chance of surviving in the sea.) The sailors threw Jonah into the sea, and the storm calmed down. But what happened next was surely something Jonah didn't expect. He was swallowed by a huge fish and was stuck inside its belly for three days and three nights. Jonah cried out to God to save him. He apologized to God for disobeying, and he promised if God saved him, he would do what God had asked and go to Nineveh. God answered Jonah's prayer. He made the fish spit Jonah out onto dry land.

Jonah did go to Nineveh and encourage the people there to behave. But Jonah kept complaining. He allowed his heart to fill with anger and bitterness.

In one of Paul's letters, he wrote, "Love does not do the wrong thing" (1 Corinthians 13:5). Doing what's wrong separates us from God's love. It leads us away from loving others with a godly kind of love. What did you learn about love from Jonah's story? Do you think there was any room left in his heart for love? Do you think Jonah really loved God?

If you know what is right to do but you do not do it, you sin.
JAMES 4:17

Dear God, I love You. Help me to do the right thing even when it's hard. . .

DAY 38
ANGER

Pop quiz: what are the top three things that make you feel angry? Everyone feels angry sometimes. If you feel tired or hungry and you can't rest or eat right away, that could make you a little angry. If your parents say no to what you want, that could allow angry feelings into your heart. You could really feel angry if you felt left out, misunderstood, or if someone hurt your feelings. Anger is another of those emotions that pushes love from your heart. Paul had something to say about that too: "Love does not get angry. Love does not remember the suffering that comes from being hurt by someone" (1 Corinthians 13:5).

One way to stop anger from filling up your heart and squeezing out the love is recognizing what anger feels like. Anger is sneaky. It can begin with a frown on your face or some angry words you say to yourself. It can grow fast like a marshmallow puffing up when you toast it in a campfire. Anger can feel like a volcano about to erupt inside you. If you can't calm it down, it will explode all over the place. Those angry words you kept to yourself might pop right out of your mouth.

When you feel angry, talk with someone about it. Talk with God. Think of some words other than "angry" that describe how you feel. You could say, "God, I'm disappointed I didn't get my way." "God, I feel frustrated because I don't understand my teacher's assignment." "God, I feel sad because I wasn't invited." Tell God all about it, and ask Him to fill up your heart with His love. Sometimes, just talking with God and knowing He loves and understands you are enough to calm your anger. Talking with a trusted adult can help too.

Paul told his friends to manage their anger before the day is done. He knew that allowing anger to stay in our hearts can lead to us doing wrong things. When you feel angry, it can help to give yourself a time-out. Ride your bike, read a book, or do something kind for someone. Fill up your heart with love.

If you are angry, do not let it become sin.
Get over your anger before the day is finished.
EPHESIANS 4:26

Dear God, please help me to manage my anger. . .

HONESTY

Paul kept on writing about love and explaining what true love is. He said, "Love is not happy with sin. Love is happy with the truth" (1 Corinthians 13:6). If Paul asked you to explain what that means, how would you answer?

The Bible verse for today, Proverbs 11:3 (NCV), says: "Good people will be guided by honesty." That means we are guided by the Holy Spirit's voice in our hearts reminding us to tell the truth. God is always truthful, and He will always lead us toward doing what is right and true.

An untruth—a lie—can be hidden in tricky language. Imagine your mom baked a big batch of oatmeal cookies. When you came home from school, you took two. You know Mom doesn't want you eating sweets before supper, but you took them anyway. That was the first sinful thing you did. Then, when your mom asked if you took a cookie, you said, "No, I didn't take one." You used tricky language to cover up a lie. You didn't take one cookie, you took *two*. Disguising the truth is dishonest.

Forgetting to mention something important can also be a lie. Say you borrowed your brother's chess game to take to a friend's house so you could teach her to play. You lost a piece. When you returned the game to your brother, you didn't tell him. That's dishonest because you purposely left out a very important piece of information.

What if you heard gossip about a classmate that you knew wasn't true and you didn't say so? Keeping the truth to yourself is another way of being dishonest.

So, you see, dishonesty is more than just telling a lie. It's twisting the truth, purposely leaving out information, and allowing others to believe something that you know isn't true.

Paul said it's a loving thing to be honest. God expects honesty from you. He is always pleased when you are truthful. When you are honest, you earn trust. People can count on you to tell the truth. Being honest makes your heart happy because it allows plenty of space in there for love.

❇

Good people will be guided by honesty; dishonesty will destroy those who are not trustworthy.
PROVERBS 11:3 NCV

Dear God, guide me to be honest.
Remind me that being dishonest is more than
telling a lie; it's twisting the truth. . .

GRACE

What if you messed up again, and again, and again? What if you messed up so many times and in so many ways you believed no one would ever trust you again or forgive you? That would zap the love right out of your heart, wouldn't it?

There is someone who loves you no matter how often you mess up. That person is God. His love for you is so great! Although God is disappointed and made sad when you disobey His rules, He forgives you all the time. God sees the best in you.

That's how God wants you to treat others. He wants you to look for the best in them, to be kind, caring, and loving even when they don't deserve it. There's a word for that: *grace.*

Grace is when you focus on the good in people instead of the ways they mess up. Maybe your baby sister is constantly taking your things without asking. You've talked with her about it, and she says she's sorry, but then she does it again. Grace would be continuing to forgive her, believing that she will eventually remember to ask, and loving her because she's your sister and she is wonderful in so many ways.

Grace is not criticizing others when they mess up. It's remembering that you mess up sometimes too. Grace is showing patience toward others and believing they are doing their best. It is accepting an apology and believing the other person means it. Grace is not being quick to judge someone's behavior. It is listening to their explanation and getting all the facts.

Paul said, "Love believes all things" (1 Corinthians 13:7). Unless you have a very good reason not to see the best in others, the loving thing to do is believe they are honest and deserving of forgiveness and trust. Grace is remembering everyone messes up—just like you. You are no better than anyone else when it comes to sin. Everyone does it. Grace is forgiving others and believing they will try harder next time to do what's right.

You must be kind to each other. Think of the other person. Forgive other people just as God forgave you.
EPHESIANS 4:32

Dear God, help me to see the best in others and to treat them with forgiveness, kindness, and love. . .

DAY 41
HOPE

Paul said, "Love hopes for all things" (1 Corinthians 13:7). Think about the people you love. What do you hope for them? You might hope that your dad finds a job, your grandma gets well, your brother wins his tennis match, your mom's car can be repaired. . . You hope for good things.

Hope means waiting for something that hasn't happened yet. Hope is being patient. It means patiently waiting for a situation to occur or to change. It is a loving thing to hope for the best for others, but it is even more loving to keep hoping even when things don't happen or change. Hope means not giving up on each other.

Say you had an older cousin who was always getting into trouble, bad trouble, the kind that made you worry. People tried to help him. They forgave him when he did wrong things. They gave him more chances to behave. Still, nothing changed. Your cousin kept messing up. You could choose to give up on him and think he would always be someone who would get into trouble, or you could hold onto hope for him. You know God loves your cousin. God doesn't want him to have a lifetime of messing up. So, you could pray and ask God for help. Even though you don't see a change right away, you can continue to hope that God is working in your cousin's life. It might take years for you to see a change, or it could happen tomorrow. You can't know God's plan. Your job is to love your cousin and hold on to hope that he stops messing up and turns his life around. Not having hope separates us from others, and it robs them of our love.

Hope is connected to something else: *faith*. Faith is believing God can do anything. It is trusting that He is working on what we hope for. Faith is waiting and believing that God will work everything out in His own way and in His own time.

Work at loving others and being hopeful for them even when it's hard. Tell them, "I love you, and I won't give up on you."

But if we hope for something we do not yet
see, we must learn how to wait for it.
ROMANS 8:25

Dear God, teach me to love with a hopeful heart. . .

HEAVEN

After Paul explained to his friends what true love was, he wrote: "Love never comes to an end" (1 Corinthians 13:8). If you think about that, you might say, "Everything on earth comes to an end." And you would be right. Everything on earth does end. Everything has a beginning and an ending except true love. Even if someone you love dies, you keep on loving them inside your heart. Right? Paul was talking about a similar kind of love—God's love. It is a love that lasts forever. God has existed forever, and God has been loving forever. The Bible even says, "God *is* love." Everything about Him is loving, and if you love God, nothing can ever separate you from His love. God will come into your heart and live there forever. Not just until your body dies—but forever!

Your hidden heart, that secret place God has tucked away inside you, doesn't die with your body. It goes on forever. Your hidden heart holds everything that makes you, you! Another name for it is your *soul*. Jesus made a way for your soul to be clean and neat when it leaves your body to go to heaven. Because of Him, you are made perfect enough for heaven. In heaven, you will have a new body for your soul to live in, a body even better than the one you have now.

Heaven is all about love. Nothing bad can exist there. Everything is perfectly perfect, just the way God is perfectly perfect. Imagine God's love shining on you like sunlight, only better. Imagine no arguing, no fighting, no sickness, no hunger, and no wanting. In heaven, you will have everything you need and more. In heaven, God pours his love over everyone and everything all the time, without end. Heaven is God's home, and He welcomes you there. You can be sure He will have all kinds of new and exciting things for you to see and do, forever!

None of us are good enough for heaven, but still, God wants us to be there with Him. Why? Because He loves us! He loves us so much that He wants us to live with Him always.

Those who do not love do not know God because God is love.
1 JOHN 4:8

Dear God, thank You for your never-ending love. . .

89

MY THOUGHTS

When you daydream, where do your thoughts take you? Do you think about something fun you're looking forward to? Or maybe your thoughts are more like wishes that take you to imaginary places. There are times when our thoughts like to go their own way. They take us where we don't want to go. That's when it's important to get them back on the right path.

How will you know if your thoughts are leading you in the wrong direction? By listening closely to what they tell you. Remember, your thoughts can come from two separate places, God's Holy Spirit or Satan. God will never lead you to think *Nothing good ever happens to me*, or *I'm not good enough*, or *Nobody loves me*. He won't lead you to think bad thoughts about others either.

The Bible says, "Let God change your life. First of all, let Him give you a new mind. Then you will know what God wants you to do. And the things you do will be good and pleasing and perfect" (Romans 12:2). When your thoughts tell you not-so-nice things or make you feel badly about yourself or others, focus on what is good and pleasing and perfect. Talk with God, and ask Him to give you a new mind.

Turning your thoughts around can be like a game. Be the first to recognize when a thought comes into your mind that is negative—a thought that says something unkind about yourself or someone else. Then, replace that thought with something positive—replace it with something good about yourself or others. For example, if a thought pops up and says, "I'm afraid I can't do this," replace it with "I've done hard things before, and I can do this too!" Or if a thought says, "I'm so angry with my sister," replace it with "I love my sister. I can't imagine my life without her." When you practice turning negative thoughts to positive, you will notice God beginning to give you a new mind.

❊

Keep your minds thinking about whatever is true, whatever is respected, whatever is right, whatever is pure, whatever can be loved, and whatever is well thought of. If there is anything good and worth giving thanks for, think about these things.
PHILIPPIANS 4:8

Dear God, please guide my thoughts
in the right direction. . .

TRUE THOUGHTS

While Paul was in prison, he kept writing letters to his friends. He wanted them to think about Jesus. Paul's thoughts took him to a time far into the future. He wrote to his friend Timothy: "There will come times of much trouble. People will love themselves and money. They will have pride and tell of all the things they have done. They will speak against God. Children and young people will not obey their parents. People will not be thankful and they will not be holy. They will not love each other. No one can get along with them. They will tell lies about others. They will not be able to keep from doing things they know they should not do. They will be wild and want to beat and hurt those who are good. They will not stay true to their friends. They will act without thinking. They will think too much of themselves. They will love fun instead of loving God" (2 Timothy 3:1–4).

Do you see any of what Paul said happening today? Much of what Paul thought about has come true. Now more than ever, it's important to keep your thoughts set on what God says is true, good, and right. Pop quiz: If people love themselves more than God and if they brag all the time about what they've done, do you think that's right? How about if they use God's name in disrespectful ways or disobey their parents? What if they're selfish and tell lies, is that good? Those people are acting without thinking. They aren't remembering all the things God says are right and true. And they aren't trying their best to be like Jesus.

Jesus said, "I am the Way and the Truth and the Life. No one can go to the Father except by Me" (John 14:6). Thinking about Jesus and doing your best to be like Him will keep your thoughts focused on the truth and what God says is right. Then, even though not-so-good things are happening in the world around you, your hidden heart will stay happy and calm.

✳

Keep your minds thinking about things in heaven.
Do not think about things on the earth.
COLOSSIANS 3:2

Dear God, please help me keep my thoughts focused on Jesus and what You've taught me to be true. . .

RESPECTFUL THOUGHTS

Being respectful is important. It is one way of acting out what Jesus taught when He said, "Do for other people whatever you would like to have them do for you" (Matthew 7:12). When you keep Jesus in your thoughts, you will remember to treat others with kindness, respect, and love.

We all know someone who is difficult to get along with. Your thoughts toward that person could turn angry. If you let any disrespectful thinking grow inside you, then you might say or do something disrespectful. But if you turn your thoughts toward Jesus, it's possible to put those angry feelings away. When you do what is good and right, you will please God and your heart will be at peace.

Maybe you have a teacher or coach who expects more from you than you think you can give. You might feel disrespect welling up inside because that person is pushing you too hard. Some of the most successful adults give credit to teachers, coaches, and other leaders who were tough on them when they were learning. Looking back, they see it was because their leaders wanted them to do well. Sometimes a teacher or coach or even your parents will push you to become even better. They have faith in you. They know you can do it! They want you to think—and believe—that you can do better. If you feel like being disrespectful toward your parents or teachers for expecting too much from you, think about the reasons they might be a little hard on you. Treat them with respect.

Can you think of two examples of what it means to be disrespectful? What do you think Jesus might tell you to do in those situations? When you think about what Jesus taught in the Bible and act in the ways He acted, you will have respect for others.

You are a respectful girl. You do your very best to be polite and use kind words when talking to and about others. When you keep Jesus and the idea of being respectful in your thoughts, then you will remember to treat others with kindness and love.

✳

The one who shows respect is always greater
than the one who receives it.
HEBREWS 7:7

Dear Jesus, please help me to be
respectful to everyone all the time. . .

I AM GOOD ENOUGH!

Imagine you have a goal to meet: getting a better grade at school, winning a competition, learning to play a musical instrument, or anything else. You try your hardest. You do your best. But you fail. You feel sad inside, and you say to yourself, "I'm not good enough." Who do you think put that thought inside your head? Not God! He will never lead you to think you aren't good enough. When you try your hardest and do your best, God will say, "Well done!"—even if you don't meet your goal.

Do you think others might not respect you if you don't succeed? Remember, you earn respect by doing your best and not necessarily by winning. You are young and still learning. Sometimes you will fail. But don't give up! Paul wrote about this in his letters. He knew he wasn't perfect. He said he had learned to forget the past and instead focus on what was ahead. Paul focused his thoughts on Jesus (Philippians 3:12–14). When you keep your thoughts on Jesus, as Paul did, Jesus will lead you away from thinking that you aren't good enough. He will remind you that the most important goal in life is to do your best to live right and please God.

Let's set a new goal today, a lifelong goal. Beginning today, make it your goal to teach others how God wants them to live. Show them by the way you talk and what you do. Set a good example. Instead of thinking so much about whether others respect you, set your thoughts on what God thinks of you. He is watching. When He sees you trying hard, doing your best, and setting a good example, you will have His respect. And you should respect yourself too! Every day, tell yourself, "I'm not perfect, but I'm trying hard and doing my best. I AM GOOD ENOUGH, and not just today but all the time."

✳

Let no one show little respect for you because you are young. Show other Christians how to live by your life. They should be able to follow you in the way you talk and in what you do. Show them how to live in faith and in love and in holy living.
1 Timothy 4:12

Dear God, I believe I am worthy of respect. . .

PURE THOUGHTS

If you live where it snows, then you know snow looks pure white and perfect when it falls. It lies like a blanket on the earth, a fresh blanket of snow with no footprints. It glistens like diamonds in sunlight. New-fallen snow is just about as pure and perfect as can be. But it doesn't stay that way. People and animals walk on it, leaving dents all over the place. The snow melts. It turns to wet, sloppy slush squishing under the soles of your boots. Trucks with plows move the snow off the streets and into mounds on the sides. Those mounds get dirty and gritty from all the cars and trucks passing by. The once beautiful pure white snow is gone. It got all messed up.

Our thoughts are somewhat like that snow. Good thoughts come to us from the Holy Spirit. They are gentle, willing, unselfish thoughts that lead us to acts of loving-kindness and doing good. Those kinds of thoughts are pure like new-fallen snow. But stuff can happen to mess up those thoughts. Satan is always whispering to us, saying things like "Do whatever you want; God's not watching." "Who cares if you use bad language sometimes or talk badly about others. Everybody does it!" "Be angry. Get even when things aren't fair." If you listen to what Satan says and do what he tells you, then your pure thoughts turn to slush. They melt away.

Everyone has impure thoughts sometimes—thoughts they know are wrong. It's because we're human and imperfect. We are pulled in two directions, good and bad. It's the way we choose that matters. If impure thoughts enter your head, don't act on them. It's that simple. Your thoughts might still try pulling you in a wrong direction, but they have no power if you don't do as they say.

Can you think of a time when you said no to an impure thought and did what was right instead?

✳

But the wisdom that comes from heaven is first of all pure. Then it gives peace. It is gentle and willing to obey. It is full of loving-kindness and of doing good. It has no doubts and does not pretend to be something it is not.
JAMES 3:17

Dear God, guide me away from impure thoughts and toward the wisdom that comes from You. . .

DAY 48
PETER'S STORY— EYES ON JESUS

The Bible says it was evening, and Jesus had just finished speaking to a huge crowd of five thousand people near the Sea of Galilee. He told His disciples to get in their boat and row to the other side of the sea. (It was a small sea. It usually would take the disciples about two hours to get to the other side.) Then Jesus went up on a mountainside to spend some quiet time praying. Meanwhile, the weather turned windy. The wind was so strong the disciples' boat was tossed around by the waves. As hard as they rowed, they weren't making much progress crossing the sea.

Jesus saw His disciples halfway across the sea working very hard to row. The boat was in trouble. It was about three o'clock in the morning. Soon, the disciples saw something. "It's a spirit!" they cried with fear. A figure was walking toward them on the waves. They heard a voice, "Take hope. It is I. Do not be afraid" (Matthew 14:27). They knew that voice. It was Jesus!

One of the disciples, Peter, said, "If it is You, Lord, tell me to come to You on the water." Jesus said, "Come!" Peter got out of the boat and stepped into the sea. He didn't sink! He walked on the water toward Jesus. But when he thought about the strong wind, he was afraid. "He began to go down in the water. He cried out, 'Lord, save me!' At once Jesus put out His hand and took hold of him. Jesus said to Peter, "You have so little faith! Why did you doubt?" (Matthew 14:28–31).

Do you think Peter would have sunk into the water if he had kept his eyes on Jesus and focused his thoughts on Jesus instead of the wind? As long as Peter focused on the Lord, he was able to do something amazing, something he thought he could never do.

You won't ever walk on water like Peter did. But if you keep your thoughts focused on Jesus, He will help you do great things. Keep your eyes on Him and your goals. Keep walking toward them, and don't be afraid.

✻

At once Jesus spoke to them and said,
"Take hope. It is I. Do not be afraid!"
MATTHEW 14:27

Dear Jesus, I will keep my eyes on
You and not be afraid. . .

DAY 49
FEAR

The Bible often repeats things. Maybe it's because God wants His messages to sink deeply into our hidden hearts. He wants us to remember to love Him and each other, to trust in Him, to be happy and have hope. One of His commands most often repeated in the Bible is "Do not be afraid." Guess how many times it appears? Did you say ten? Fifty? A hundred? "Do not be afraid" is in the Bible 365 times! Maybe that number is no accident. There are 365 days in a year. Could God want to remind us every day that because He loves us and because He is the one and only true God, we don't have to be afraid?

What are you afraid of? Maybe just thinking about what scares you makes you a little jittery. No scary thing has any power over you because God is bigger and greater than what makes you feel afraid. Spiders, snakes, and bees? God made them, and He has power over them all. Thunder, lightning, floods, and wind? God has command over the weather too. Whatever frightens you, God says, "Do not be afraid." When you remember that and keep your thoughts focused on Him, God will provide you with courage to stand up to whatever gets in your way.

When Moses was afraid to go to Egypt's pharaoh and tell him, "God says, 'Let my people go,'" God provided Moses with courage. God did the same for Esther when she was afraid to tell King Ahasuerus that she was a Jew. God gave Shadrach, Meshach, and Abednego courage when King Nebuchadnezzar sentenced them to die in a fiery furnace. And God will give you courage too. Whenever you feel afraid, put your trust in Him. Say a prayer and ask God to help you stay calm. Then listen for the Holy Spirit's voice inside your heart telling you to stay calm and trust God. God loves you. His Spirit is always with you. If you believe that and trust in God's power, you will know you are not alone, and you never have to be afraid.

For God did not give us a spirit of fear. He gave us a spirit of power and of love and of a good mind.
2 TIMOTHY 1:7

Dear God, You are always with me. I will not be afraid. . .

METAMORPHOSIS

Metamorphosis. It could be a new word for you, or maybe you've learned it in school. It means "a great change in appearance or character." A caterpillar changes in appearance when it transitions into a butterfly. People change in character especially as they get older and become wiser.

You've reached Day 50 of these 100 days of devotionals. It's the halfway point. Have you begun a metamorphosis? You likely haven't changed much in appearance—that would be weird. You are still the beautiful, amazing, smart girl you were when you began reading this book. But have you noticed a change in your character?

Here are some questions to think about. As you've learned more about who God is, have you formed a closer relationship with Him? How about prayer, has the way you pray changed? Are you more likely now to tell God everything, knowing He will forgive you when you mess up? Do you trust God to be with you all the time? Have you become wiser about how He wants you to live?

If you are putting into action some or all of what you've learned, then you are likely noticing some changes in yourself. You might be more patient now, less afraid, or more courageous. Maybe you are getting along better with others and especially those who are difficult to get along with. Are you more helpful now? Are you being kind and loving toward others even when they don't deserve it? Think about it. How have you changed as you've tried even harder to live in ways that please God?

It could be you haven't noticed many changes yet. Some caterpillars take only a week or two to become butterflies while others take years. If you want your character to change to please God, put your faith in Jesus. Ask Him to teach you about what pleases God and to become more like Him. Don't give up. You've just begun to learn. God wants you to keep reading and keep learning and most of all to put into action what you've learned.

✱

For if a man belongs to Christ, he is a new person.
The old life is gone. New life has begun.
2 Corinthians 5:17

Dear Jesus, I want to change. I want to know more about You and how God wants me to live. Help me to become more like You. . .

ACTiON!

Imagine that you are an actor on a movie set about to film a scene. You and others in the scene are in your costumes and makeup. You know your lines. You are ready and waiting for the director to say, "*Aaaaaaaaand, ACTION!*" But all he says is, "*Aaaaaaaaand. . .*" There's no command to act. You and the others are left standing like statues, ready but doing nothing. What good is it if you say you are actors, but you do nothing to prove it?

Jesus' half-sibling, James, wrote one of the books in the Bible. In it he asked a similar question, "What good does it do if you say you have faith but do not do things that prove you have faith?" (James 2:14). James meant God wants us to prove we have faith in Him by obeying Him and serving others—by taking action. Otherwise, we are like actors standing still on a movie set waiting for someone to tell us what to do.

James said, "What if a [person] does not have clothes or food? And one of you says to him, 'Goodbye, keep yourself warm and eat well.' But if you do not give him what he needs, how does that help him?" (James 2:15–16). Think about that: What would you do if your friend only had the clothes she was wearing? What if she had nothing to eat? Would you tell her, "Stay warm and eat well," or would you take action and help her get the clothes and food she needs? If you did what Jesus would have done and helped your friend, that is putting faith into action! God will lead you to where there's a need. He will bring you to someone who requires help. And then God will say in your hidden heart, "Action!" You have the choice to obey Him and do something, or you can walk away.

Each day, we hear about people helping others. Sometimes help comes in small ways, other times it's heroic. No matter how big or small, helping is taking action. By being God's helpers here on earth, we prove our faith to Him. We show God that we love Him.

A faith that does not do things is a dead faith.
JAMES 2:17

Dear God, I'm ready to act. Show me what to do. . .

DAY 52
NEHEMiAH

The Bible tells of Nehemiah, a Jewish man from Jerusalem living a good life in Persia. When his brother and a few Jewish friends came to visit him, Nehemiah asked, "So, what's going on in Jerusalem?" His heart was broken when they said, "Jerusalem is a mess." An army of its enemies destroyed Jerusalem's walls and gates. Without a wall protecting their city, the Jews living there were in great danger. Nehemiah could have said, "I'm sorry for your trouble. I hope the wall gets rebuilt soon." That would have been easy. But instead, Nehemiah acted. He was working then for the Persian king. He went to the king and asked to be released from his duties. Then Nehemiah hurried to Jerusalem.

This is how Nehemiah described what he did first: "I got up in the night. . . . I did not tell anyone what my God was putting into my mind to do for Jerusalem. There was no animal with me except the one I was sitting on. . . . I looked at the walls of Jerusalem which were broken down and its gates which were destroyed by fire. Then I went on to the Well Gate and the King's Pool, but there was no place for the animal I was on to pass. So I went up in the night by the valley and looked at the wall. Then I went in through the Valley Gate again and returned" (Nehemiah 2:12–15). After that first sleepless night and seeing what needed to be done, Nehemiah gathered the people together—people with many different skills. He put together a team and everyone got to work. It was a huge project. There were no machines to help; still, with Nehemiah supervising, the wall was rebuilt in just 52 days!

If parts of your city were destroyed, maybe by a flood, storm, or other disaster, what could you do to help? You might say, "I'm just a kid, there's nothing I can do." Or you could get busy and pick up trash or donate food and clothing. Can you think of more ways to help?

Then they said, "Let us get up and build."
So they put their hands to the good work.
NEHEMIAH 2:18

Dear God, open my eyes to ways I can help my community. Although I'm young, I can still be a helper. . .

DAY 53
A LITTLE HELP

Today's Bible verse says, "Help each other in troubles and problems." There are many ways to help. You might be better at some than others.

Maybe you are physically strong. You love sports and working out. You love to dance and could dance all night if your parents allowed it. You have endurance—lasting strength. If you had to, you could continue for hours with few breaks in between. If you're that kind of girl, you can put your physical strength to work helping others. Your grandparents or other older adults you know could use some help with carrying, lifting, or moving heavier items, cleaning, or doing yard work. That's something you can do! Get your body moving and volunteer to help.

Or maybe you are a girl with great ideas. You see unique ways to get things done, and you're great at explaining just what to do. If you see a younger sibling or anyone else struggling to figure out how to accomplish a task, you can help by offering suggestions. Your great idea could be just what's needed. Bonus if you offer suggestions with a smile and you choose words that don't make you sound bossy or like a know-it-all.

You might be the girl whose hidden heart has a special connection with others. You understand how others feel to a point where you almost feel their feelings. If you sense something is bothering someone, you are the one who is ready to listen patiently. You don't offer advice unless asked, but you are first to offer a hug or to say, "I understand. What do you

110

need?" Sometimes, quiet help and just being there are the best kinds of help.

When you pray, ask God to show you the special helping skills He has given you. Then put those skills to work. Keep your eyes and ears open for those who could use a little help. You will find them all around you. There are people everywhere who need just the kind of help you have to offer.

*Help each other in troubles and problems. This
is the kind of law Christ asks us to obey.*
GALATIANS 6:2

Dear God, I know You created me to be a helper.
Show me the kinds of help I'm good at. Then
teach me to put my skills into action. . .

"THANK YOU"

You are a helper in many ways, but sometimes you're the one who needs help. Think about it. Can you name at least one time in the past week when you've needed help? Everyone needs help. Even Jesus had helpers. Twelve men, His disciples, traveled with Jesus. They helped with the crowds when Jesus preached. They willingly and unselfishly served Jesus, always ready to meet His needs and do whatever He asked.

Who would you call for help if there were a fire, if you got hurt, or if you saw a crime happening? Firefighters, police officers, paramedics, doctors, nurses. . . These community helpers are always ready. In the most dangerous situations, they risk their lives to save yours. There are many other helpers in your community: teachers, bus drivers, mail carriers, babysitters, cooks, pastors. . . Can you think of several more?

Your parents have helped you from the moment you were born. Imagine if, on the day you were born, everyone expected you to figure out for yourself how to do things. That's a silly thought, isn't it? Babies are helpless. Babies can't feed themselves, change their own diapers, or meet any of their other needs. They need their parents' help. Others in the family join in as helpers—grandparents, aunts, and uncles. Older family members are all around, helping you to grow up. They are there when you want help and sometimes even when you don't. Your family members love you, and they would do anything for you.

Your friends and siblings are your helpers too. If anyone dares to say anything bad about you or otherwise gets in your way, your brothers, sisters, and best friends will be loyal and stick with you no matter what.

The help we receive from others can become so familiar and ordinary that sometimes we forget to be appreciative and say, "Thank you." God set all these special helpers in your life. It's important to thank Him for those who help. It's also important to get in the habit of thanking your helpers and praying for them too. When was the last time you thanked your mom, dad, sister, brother, or friend? Be sure to say "thank you" today.

✱

I always give thanks for you and pray for you.
EPHESIANS 1:16

Dear God, thank You for all my helpers. . .

DAY 55
HELPING THE WORLD

Your eyes are open to the world's problems, and you dream of making the world a better place. Your goal might be to help by using medicine to heal people, or maybe you want to explore new ways to save the environment or make cities and schools safer. It could be that you don't know yet exactly how you want to help, but you know when you grow up, you will do something to help the world.

There's one thing you can do right now. It doesn't require any special training. All you need is to love Jesus and believe that He came to save the world from sin. Remember: God allowed Jesus to take into His heart all the sinful things people would ever do. Jesus took the punishment for the sins everyone would ever commit. God promised that anyone who trusted in Jesus and asked for forgiveness for their sins would be forgiven. Their hidden hearts would be made perfectly clean and ready for heaven when they died. Before Jesus left earth to go back to heaven, He told His followers, "Go to all the world and preach the Good News to every person" (Mark 16:15). You can do what Jesus said, and right now, today, start spreading the news.

You don't have to go to other countries and not even to other states or cities. You can begin with your family and friends. You can tell them about Jesus and why He died on the cross. You can share with them all the wonderful things you love about Jesus and why He is so special to you. Tell them you want to share Jesus with the whole world, and ask them to help you by telling others about Him.

Imagine, if you tell someone about Jesus, and she tells someone, and that person tells someone else, and on and on. Eventually, your message might reach all around the world. As more people learn about Jesus and do their best to do what is right and pleasing to Him, you can be sure the world will become a better place.

He said to them, "You are to go to all the world and preach the Good News to every person."
Mark 16:15

Dear Jesus, I want to be Your helper.
I'm ready to share the Good News. . .

BE BOLD!

After Jesus went back to heaven, His followers had a hard time. There were people who still didn't believe Jesus was God's Son. They didn't like Jesus' followers sharing the news that Jesus had made a way for everyone to go to heaven. Jesus' followers had a choice. They could keep the good news to themselves and live without others giving them trouble, or they could do what Jesus said and share the good news. They chose Jesus.

Being a Jesus-follower isn't always easy. People who don't believe in God might make fun of those who do. If a Jesus-follower decides not to join in an activity because the Bible says it's wrong, she could be left behind while her friends do it anyway. True followers of Jesus choose to do what's right even when it's difficult or unpopular. True Jesus-followers are bold. That means they are courageous and confident. They are sure Jesus is the Son of God, and they are courageous when talking about Him and doing what is right.

Are you bold? If a friend wanted you to do something you knew was wrong, would you say, "No." Sometimes, it takes courage to say no. Courage is a good thing! Not everyone has it. Standing against what you know is wrong could end with others laughing at your decisions or going their own way and leaving you behind. That might hurt your feelings. But remember that Jesus is always with you. He loves it when you boldly stand up for Him and for everything that is right.

Jesus' followers, Peter and John, were put in jail for speaking about Jesus. That didn't stop them. They prayed, " 'Now, Lord, consider their threats and enable your servants to speak your word with great boldness.' . . . And they were all filled with the Holy Spirit and spoke the word of God boldly" (Acts 4:29, 31 NIV). Whenever you need courage to stand up for Jesus and what is right, talk with God. He will give you the courage you need.

I am not ashamed of the Good News. It is the power of God. It is the way He saves men from the punishment of their sins if they put their trust in Him.
ROMANS 1:16

Dear God, help me to be bold and
stand up for what's right. . .

DAY 57
ACQUAINTANCES AND FRIENDS

Today's Bible verse is a reminder to choose your friends carefully. Many people will come into your life, but you get to choose who will become your friends. Proverbs 12:26 also warns against choosing friends who will lead you astray—friends who will lead you away from Jesus and doing what is right.

Before you invite someone into your life as a friend, think about these questions: Am I comfortable talking with this person about Jesus and what I believe is right? Does she know Jesus and make choices that please Him? Will this person encourage me to do what's right? Will she stand up for me even if it's unpopular? Would Jesus be pleased with how this person talks and acts? Who does this person choose as her friends; would I want to be friends with them? If you answered yes to these questions, you would be making a wise choice about accepting this person as a friend. It sounds as if you two have a lot in common. You might even become the best of friends.

There is a difference between being a friend and being an acquaintance. A friend is someone you choose; an acquaintance is someone you know. Popularity is super important to some people. They don't care how they choose their friends as much as they care how many friends they have. If popularity is their goal, they might not care about following others down a wrong path. But you are different! You know Jesus, and you choose

118

your friends wisely. You have many acquaintances—people you know—and you are nice to them. The ways you talk and act might lead them nearer to Jesus. When they see the good example you set, they might even want to become your friend. Be welcoming, caring, and kind toward everyone. But remember that true friends are more like sisters and brothers. They share your values. They love you and will be there to support and encourage you all the time, no matter what.

Ask God to help choose your friends. Then keep your eyes open. Those God-chosen friends are out there, and at just the right times God will bring you together.

✽

The righteous choose their friends carefully,
but the way of the wicked leads them astray.
PROVERBS 12:26 NIV

Dear God, I want You to help me choose my friends. . .

FiTTiNG IN

Do you think Jesus was popular? Many people saw the miracles He did. At a wedding reception, Jesus changed water into wine. He fed a crowd of five thousand people with just five loaves of bread and two fish. Jesus healed the sick. He even brought people back to life again after they were dead. Many people were curious about Jesus and what He said about God and living right. Soon, huge crowds followed wherever He went. But did all those people truly believe Jesus was the Son of God? Jesus was different from most. He was popular, yes, but when the leaders turned against Jesus and had Him arrested and when Jesus was sentenced to die on the cross, many followers left Him. They were afraid to support Him and His unpopular ideas.

Before Jesus was arrested, He said to His disciples, "If you find the godless world is hating you, remember it got its start hating me. If you lived on the world's terms, the world would love you as one of its own. But since I picked you to live on God's terms and no longer on the world's terms, the world is going to hate you" (John 15:18–19 MSG). Jesus knew His followers might not always fit in or be popular.

If you choose to follow Jesus, you know you will fit in with other Jesus-followers. But because you follow Jesus, you might be unpopular with those who choose sin over what is right and good. Everyone wants to fit in. Following the crowd is the easy thing to do. But choosing to do what's right isn't always easy.

There will be times when you feel you don't fit in—and that's okay. You know who you are: God's girl! You live to please Him, and He gives you courage to stand out from the crowd. Jesus doesn't want you to become more like the world. He wants you to become more like Him.

Do you feel okay with not fitting in if it means becoming more like Jesus?

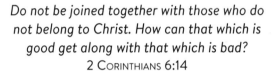

Do not be joined together with those who do not belong to Christ. How can that which is good get along with that which is bad?
2 Corinthians 6:14

Dear God, when I feel like I don't fit in, remind me that I always fit in with You. . .

HOW TO TALK WITH YOUR PARENTS (AND OTHER TRUSTED ADULTS)

The Bible says to honor your father and mother. What do you think "honor" means? Did you say, "to obey them"? Obeying your parents is one way of honoring them. But just as much, honoring your mom and dad means showing that you trust them. You trust your parents to provide you with food and shelter, to keep you safe, to help you stay healthy, and to be sure you get an education. It's good to recognize those things and thank your parents for them. But there's another way to show you trust your mom and dad. It's likely one you haven't thought of. You can honor your parents by talking with them—*really* talking with them about what's bothering you, your everyday thoughts, things you wonder about, and your hopes and dreams. Opening up and sharing your thoughts with your parents will make them feel wonderful knowing you trust them enough to tell them anything.

Get in the habit of talking with your mom and dad. Put away your electronics, sit down, and have conversations. You might even tell them you'd like to set aside a special time each day to talk, maybe just before bedtime or while taking a walk together. Be brave about sharing your thoughts without worrying how your parents might react. Plan what you want to say. Even plan your response if you and your parents disagree.

Be prepared not to get angry or walk away. Tell Mom and Dad how you feel. Listen, and if you don't understand, ask questions. Having real conversations with your parents builds trust, and the more you trust each other, the more likely your mom and dad will be to allow you more responsibility.

Talking about Jesus and your faith in God is always a good conversation starter. Does your family pray together? Ask your parents to pray with you and also to pray for specific things that concern you. If they know your problems, thoughts, and goals, your parents can talk with God about those things during their own quiet times in prayer.

Give it a try today. Sit down with Mom and Dad and have a conversation.

✳

"Honor your father and your mother."
EXODUS 20:12

Dear God, please teach me how to have
good conversations with my parents
and other trusted adults. . .

"I'M SO STRESSED OUT!"

What a day you've had! You missed the school bus (again!). Your mom was late for work because she had to drive you to school. Then you remembered you forgot your lunch. Your dad had to bring it to you during his work break. Your teacher gave the class a surprise quiz on the social studies chapter you were supposed to read, the one you just sort of skimmed over. That didn't go well. Then you and your best friend had an argument, and now you two aren't speaking. The ride home on the bus was awkward. You've had a bad day. It's all just too much, and you're stressed out. The day isn't over yet, and you wonder how much more stress will be dumped on you before bedtime.

Stress is that feeling that builds up inside you and slowly inflates like a balloon. It makes your muscles feel tight. It might even give you a headache. Stress can build and build until you feel like you're going to pop! When you feel stressed out, how do you handle it? Do you hold it all inside or let it out in an angry outburst? Neither of those things is healthy. Find someplace where you can be alone. Take some deep breaths and be quiet for a while. God says, "Be quiet and know that I am God" (Psalm 46:10). Take time to pray and tell Him about your bad day. Ask God to help you calm down. Give your troubles to Him.

Some stress can't be avoided. It's part of life. A little stress is normal. It can teach you to be patient, to solve problems, focus on your work, and to meet challenges with strength. A little stress can be helped by making a schedule and sticking to it, thinking ahead, and being prepared, by breaking down big tasks into chunks, and even by exercising to blow off steam. Dance, sing, play. . .

It's not good when stress gets big and is caused by too much to do, problems in school, a sudden change, or someone treating you badly. Talk with your mom and dad or another trusted grown-up. Tell them what's going on, and ask them to help you.

Be quiet and know that I am God.
Psalm 46:10

Dear God, please quiet me as we
spend some time together. . .

DAY 61
"I NEED SOME SPACE"

Is your world sometimes a little too "people-y" with sisters, brothers, parents, teachers, friends, coaches. . .all kinds of people wanting a piece of your time? Do you wish all those people would just go away and give you a little space?

You might be surprised that Jesus felt that way too. Wherever He went, His disciples traveled with Him, learning from Him and asking questions. Huge crowds followed Him, wanting things from Him. Part of Jesus' work here on earth was speaking to large crowds. Sometimes, Jesus just wanted to get away from them, to be alone in a private place where He could pray and rest for a while. The Bible says when Jesus learned that His cousin, John, died, He wanted to be alone, but still people followed Him (Matthew 14:13). Even when Jesus did find a place to be alone, people interrupted Him (Matthew 17:19, 24:3). One day, after Jesus had spoken to a crowd of thousands and gave them all a meal, He sent the people away. He told His disciples to take the boat and sail to the town of Bethsaida ahead of Him. Then, finally with everyone gone, Jesus went up to the mountain alone to pray (Mark 6:45–46).

Do you have a special place where you can be alone? It's okay sometimes to want to send all the people away so you can rest, think, and pray. If finding an alone place is difficult, talk with your parents and tell them how you feel. Ask them to suggest places where you can be by yourself and not interrupted. You might want to share with them what you've learned about Jesus needing alone time too.

When you get the space you need, use that time wisely. Turn your thoughts away from your worries. Be quiet and listen for God's voice inside your hidden heart. Be still. Rest, and try to tune out the noise around you. Jesus understands you need space sometimes. In heaven, Jesus doesn't need to rest anymore. He is with you all the time. Jesus wants to spend time with you and hear your prayers.

❋

In the morning before the sun was up, Jesus went to a place where He could be alone. He prayed there.
MARK 1:35

Dear Jesus, I need a little space today. . .

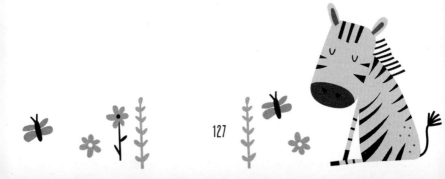

CURRENT EVENTS

There is always much going on in the world. You might hear your parents discussing current events—things happening in your community, state, nation, and other countries around the world. Some of what you hear might trouble you. That's normal. The world, whether your little piece of it or the whole thing, is constantly busy and changing. When a lot of news comes at you all at once, it can make you feel anxious. So, what can you do to calm yourself? You can take your eyes off the world and focus just on today.

King David wrote, "This is the day that the Lord has made. Let us be full of joy and be glad in it" (Psalm 118:24). David knew that God, the great Creator, gives us each day as a new beginning. Every day is a do-over, a chance to let go of yesterday's troubles and move forward with hope that this new day will be awesome. David also knew that God fills each new day with joyful blessings—little things that make us glad. Think about this day so far. Have you experienced any of His joyful blessings? Did you see or hear something that made you smile, laugh, or made you say, "Aw, how sweet"?

Do you remember what Paul wrote about thoughts? He said, "Keep your minds thinking about whatever is true, whatever is respected, whatever is right, whatever is pure, whatever can be loved, and whatever is well thought of. If there is anything good and worth giving thanks for, think about these things"

(Philippians 4:8). Each day, you can get your eyes off the world by following Paul's good advice.

Jesus lived here on earth for a while, and even then, the world had troubles. Jesus understood that current events could make people feel a little nervous. This is what He had to say: "In the world you will have much trouble. But take hope! I have power over the world!" (John 16:33). Every day, Jesus has power over all those worldly things that bother you. So, take your eyes off the world. Focus on Jesus and be joyful and glad. Jesus has absolutely everything under control.

❉

This is the day that the Lord has made.
Let us be full of joy and be glad in it.
PSALM 118:24

Dear God, thank You for this brand-new day. . .

DAY 63
UNANSWERED PRAYERS

Is there a specific thing you are asking God to do or provide for you, but so far you haven't received it? Don't stop asking!

Jesus told His disciples this story. There was a judge who didn't care about God or the townspeople. When they came to him for help, he didn't do anything. There was one woman, though, who had been treated unfairly, and she insisted the judge do something. She went to him again and again until finally, just to stop her from bothering him, the judge gave her what she wanted. Jesus said, "Listen to what the unfair judge [did]. God will always give what is right to his people who cry to him night and day, and he will not be slow to answer them" (Luke 18:6–7 NCV).

Your idea of "slow" and God's might be different, but you can be sure if you ask God for help, He will help you. Keep praying and don't give up. Help will come, but maybe in a way different from what you expect.

When you ask for something in prayer, God won't give you what He knows wouldn't be good for you. It might not be good for you right now, or it might not be good for you in the future. God knows best what you need. This is when unanswered prayer gets a little tricky. You can't know what God has in mind for you. So, when you ask, you need to have faith that God hears you. He might not give you what you ask for, but He will always give you exactly what is right and what you need.

Finally, patience is super-important if your prayer goes unanswered. God hears every prayer, and He starts working on each one right away. He will answer every prayer in His own time and way. There may be something you want right now, but God has something even better planned for you in the future. In time, He will lead you from what you want toward that better thing. Only God can decide how to answer your prayer. He wants you to trust Him.

We are sure that if we ask anything that He wants us to have, He will hear us.
1 JOHN 5:14

Dear God, help me to be patient and trust You when I pray. . .

DAY 64
YES, NO, WE'LL SEE

In your relationship with your parents, you do a lot of asking. You ask your parents for things all the time. "Mom, may I sleep over at my friend's house?" "Dad, can we get a dog?" "Mom and Dad, could I switch to a different school next year?" Some asks are little, and others are big. Your parents might answer, "Yes." But sometimes they will say, "No" or "We'll see."

Your prayer relationship with God is much like that. You ask Him for little things and big things. Sometimes you get a yes or no answer right away. For example, if you asked God to allow your team to win Saturday's soccer match and they did, you would have received an answer to your prayer. God said, "Yes." The same would be true if your team didn't win the game. You had your answer. God said "No." You might not understand God's reason for saying no, but you accept that He has decided.

Many times, God will answer with "We'll see." Usually that comes as a response to a big ask, like asking Him to heal someone's sickness or to help your mom find an affordable apartment for your family to rent. God has a plan, and just like any good plan, it takes time. God already has the answer you are waiting for, but He isn't ready yet to share it with you.

When your parents' answer to a big ask is "We'll see," what do you do? Do you wait a while and then ask again? Do you keep asking, hoping you will get a yes or no answer? It's okay to do that when you ask God for something. Keep asking for

Him to answer yes or no. Also, listen for God's voice in your hidden heart. He might guide you to pray differently about your ask, or He might lead you toward asking for something else.

Prayer is one of the great mysteries about God. He wants us to ask. He hears and promises to answer. But we can't know how He will answer or when. We just need to have faith that He will.

He will call upon Me, and I will answer him.
PSALM 91:15

Dear God, I know You hear me and will answer my prayer. Guide me to pray according to Your will. . .

DAY 65
I DON'T UNDERSTAND

Imagine you wanted to go on a camping trip with your best friend and her family, but your dad said, "No." He gave you no reason, and when you wanted to discuss it, you weren't pleased when Dad said, "I just don't think it's a good idea." Not understanding your dad's decision made you feel angry.

Maybe your dad had some information he didn't want to share with you that helped him to make his decision. Dad is in charge, and he makes the rules. He will always do what's best for you. But sometimes, Dad knows stuff that for his own good reasons he doesn't want to share. He wants you to trust him that the decision he made is right.

The same is true with God. He is our heavenly Father, the Father of us all. God makes the rules, and He will always do what is best for His children. We might not be happy with what He decides, but God does not want us to lose faith that His decisions are right.

People sometimes get angry with God when they don't understand His decisions. If God doesn't give them what they pray for, it can be hard to understand when He says, "No." Bad things happen sometimes, and people get angry because they know God could have stopped it. It's hard for them to understand why God allowed it to happen. It's normal for people to feel angry with God when they don't understand His reasons.

When God does something you don't understand and you feel angry with Him, go to Him and pray. Talk with Him about how you feel. Ask Him to forgive you for being angry with Him. Ask God to give you peace and even strength to get past the bad thing that happened. Continue your relationship with Him. Ask your heavenly Father to heal your hurt, help you let go of your anger, and if possible, to have some understanding of His reasons. God understands all your feelings, even your anger toward Him. Try to remember all the good things God has done for you and praise Him.

Jesus answered him, "You do not understand now what I am doing but you will later."
JOHN 13:7

Dear God, why did You say no? Why did You allow that to happen? I don't understand. . .

I'D RATHER NOT

Name a job you'd rather not do. Maybe you said you'd rather not clean your cat's litter box, or pick up your room, or do your homework assignments. It would be nice to say, "I'd rather not," and move along. But that's not how life works. When you were a baby, you had no responsibilities. As you got older, your parents expected you to do your share—pick up your toys, clean your room, set the table, help with the dishes, or take out the trash. The older you get, the more responsibilities you have. There's always work to be done, and if everyone said, "I'd rather not," the world would be one gigantic mess!

So, how do you react when you face a task you'd rather not do? Do you put it off for as long as you can? Do you try to bargain your way out of doing it by trading the task for something your brother or sister wants from you? When all else fails and you're stuck doing the work, do you grumble and complain?

Paul offered some great advice for when you have a job you'd rather not do. He said, "Do it for the Lord and not for men" (Colossians 3:23). In other words, Paul suggested you imagine Jesus asking you to do the work for Him. If Jesus asked you to do the work, how would you respond? Would you drag your feet, grumble, and complain? What if Jesus' disciples had done that or said, "We'd rather not"? No one in the world would know about Jesus and the good news that He made a way for us to live forever in heaven. "Whatever work you do, do it with all your heart" (Colossians 3:23). That's what Paul said! Whatever it is—a difficult homework assignment, picking up trash, cleaning the guinea pig cage, making your bed, pulling weeds, sweeping the floor—do it with all your heart as if doing it for the Lord.

Think about that as you go about your work today. Adjust your attitude away from "I'd rather not" and toward "Jesus, I'm doing this for You."

Whatever work you do, do it with all your heart. Do it for the Lord and not for men.
COLOSSIANS 3:23

Dear Jesus, whatever work I do today, I'll do it willingly for You. . .

DAY 67
I'M NOT A FAN

Fill in the blank: I'm not a fan of _____. What first came to your mind? Maybe you aren't a fan of a certain sports team, song, movie, or game. Everyone has something they aren't a fan of, and usually they aren't afraid to say so. If someone asked, "Do you like Brussels sprouts?" and you weren't a fan, you probably wouldn't hesitate to say something like "No! I'm not a fan of those disgusting little cabbage things!" or "Eww, I'm not into them."

How about sin? Are you a fan of that? You've been learning that sin is anything that doesn't please God. It's not only big things like stealing, killing, and cheating. It can be sinful little things too: allowing a bad word to slip out, twisting the truth into a little lie, or saying something not so nice about someone behind her back. In God's eyes, there is no difference between a little sin and a big one. Sin is sin, and God is not a fan. He doesn't want you to be a fan either. That's why it's important to know right from wrong and not be afraid to say, "Not a fan," to sin.

It can take courage to say no, especially when those you are with want to do something you know is wrong. When you decide to say no, you also get to choose how to say it. You don't always have to be firm and say something like "No! I think what you're doing is sinful and displeasing to God, and I'm not going to do it." Instead, you could suggest another activity, you could simply say, "I'm not into that" or you could just walk away. Your friends might not be pleased with you if you say no to them. But God will be pleased with you. He will see you doing exactly what His Son, Jesus, would do. And when you are right with God in the same way Jesus is, God sees, and He is happy.

❀

My children, let no one lead you in the wrong way.
The man who does what is right, is right with God
in the same way as Christ is right with God.
1 JOHN 3:7

Dear God, I'm not a fan of sin. Help me to recognize it, say no to it, and push it away. . .

COMPROMISE

One definition of "compromise" is when two sides give up some of what they want to meet in the middle. For example: On school nights, your mom wants you in bed by 8:30 p.m. You want your bedtime moved to 9:30 p.m., but your mom won't agree. The two of you decide to compromise on a 9:00 p.m. bedtime. It's not exactly what either of you wanted, but you reached an agreement that works for you both.

When you were little, you and your siblings probably argued over things like sharing your toys, who got to go first, and who got the biggest scoop of ice cream. As you got older, you learned you had to compromise. You had to give a little to keep the peace or to get at least some of what you wanted. In that way, compromise is a good thing. Learning to compromise is an important skill and one you will use throughout your life.

There is another definition for "compromise." It means giving up what you know is good for something you know is bad. You should never compromise with sin—not even a little. Imagine your teacher gives you a story problem to solve for your homework assignment. Math isn't your best subject, and the story problem is hard. You've tried your best to figure it out, but you can't. You know someone who will give you the answer. A little voice in your hidden heart says, "That would be cheating, and cheating is wrong." Another voice whispers in your head, "But you tried to solve it. It's okay to give in."

Think about it: if you cheated to get the answer, that would be compromising with sin.

It's important to listen for the Holy Spirit's voice in your heart guiding you in the right direction. Satan will say things like "Go ahead. Everybody else is doing it," or "Do it just this once," or "God will forgive you." Don't listen to him! His words will always lead you away from God and into trouble.

Can you think of an example of a good kind of compromise? How about an example of when compromise isn't good?

They do not compromise with evil,
and they walk only in his paths.
Psalm 119:3 NLT

Dear God, lead me to compromise when it is good, but never to compromise with sin. . .

DON'T MOVE MY BOUNDARY MARKER!

The Old Testament in the Bible tells about God's people, the Israelites, and their long journey from slavery to a special piece of land God promised them. The land was God's gift to the Israelites, but getting there was a long and tiresome trip. It took the Israelites forty years to walk from Egypt to the land called Canaan, and there was much trouble along the way. When they finally got to their land and took it as their own, they had to fight to keep it. Their enemies kept trying to cross their boundary markers—the imaginary lines that marked the Israelites' property—and take the land as their own.

A boundary marker is a dividing line. Maybe you play games where if you cross a boundary line, there are consequences. Crossing the line breaks the rules.

Do you know you've set boundary markers for your behavior? You've made a set of rules for yourself about what is right and wrong. You've created imaginary behavior lines that you won't cross. You've set boundaries about what is right and wrong for things like your personal space and the kinds of touch you will accept as good and not good. You've set boundaries for the kinds of information you will share with others and how you will allow others to treat you. If you think about it, you've set many boundary markers that are yours alone and that you don't want others to cross.

Sometimes, Satan will try to get you to cross your own boundary markers and step out of what's right and into sin. If you aren't careful, you might compromise and move your boundary marker to allow a little bit of sin inside. Once sin takes a little, it wants a lot. Like the Israelites' enemies, it will keep trying to sneak farther beyond your boundary lines.

God gives you the gift of knowing right from wrong. Using that gift to set boundaries for yourself is important, and so is protecting them. Don't allow anyone to cross your lines and take from you what you know is right and good.

❃

Don't move a boundary marker set up by your ancestors.
PROVERBS 22:28 CEV

Dear God, guide me to set behavior boundaries
for myself. Help me to protect those boundaries
and do what is right and good. . .

DAY 70
"NEVER WiLL I EVER!"

Jesus and His twelve disciples were celebrating the festival of Passover. They were sharing a meal when Jesus told them what would happen later that night. He said, "One of you will hand Me over [to my enemies]" (Matthew 26:21). The disciples looked at one another, wondering who would do that. But one of them knew. Judas had already decided to turn Jesus in. Then Jesus told them more of what would happen. "All of you will be ashamed of Me and leave Me tonight" (v. 31). *Never will I ever!* Jesus' disciple Peter thought. He was loyal to His friend, Jesus. Peter said, "Even if all men give up and turn away because of You, I will never." But Jesus knew better. He answered Peter, "For sure, I tell you, before a rooster crows this night, you will say three times you do not know Me." Peter thought, *No way!* He said to Jesus, "Even if I have to die with You, I will never say I do not know You" (vv. 33–35). But Jesus knew better—He always does. Later that night when the soldiers came to arrest Jesus, His disciples were afraid and ran away. By the time the rooster crowed the next morning, Peter had told people three times that he did not know Jesus. Peter had messed up. He messed up big time, and he was sorry. The Bible says, "Peter went outside and cried with loud cries" (v. 75).

Do you think Jesus forgave Peter? Jesus forgives anyone who is sorry and asks for forgiveness. He wanted so much for us to be forgiven when we mess up that He suffered and died on the cross so all our sins would be forgiven. For sure,

Jesus forgave Peter for messing up. Peter didn't mean to turn against Jesus. Fear made him do it. He gave in to sin believing that, because he was Jesus' friend, he might be arrested too.

Like Peter, you might say, "Never will I ever," to sin and then mess up and feel sorry. Jesus will forgive you if you ask. He loves you like He loved Peter. Even if you messed up a hundred times, Jesus would go on loving and forgiving you.

"I have loved you just as My Father has loved Me."
John 15:9

Dear Jesus, thank You for forgiving me. . .

DAY 71
LEFT OUT

You are the kind of girl who can tell if something is bothering someone. What if, one day, you noticed your younger brother was acting quiet and sad. "What's wrong?" you ask him. Holding back tears, trying to be brave, he shares with you what happened. "We were playing basketball," he says, "and I'm shorter than the other kids. So, they kept stealing the ball from me and not letting me try to make a basket. I know I miss a lot. But, still, I wanted to try. I felt left out!" Then your little brother starts to sob, "Everybody hates me!"

What would you do? Of course, you would give your brother a hug and reassure him that nobody hates him. It is wrong to hate anybody. And you might even tell your brother that if anyone even tried to hate him, they would have to answer to you. You are an awesome sister and friend!

Maybe you know what it feels like to be left out of an activity. Remembering how you felt helped you to help your brother. Feeling left out is normal for most kids. There are times when you are growing up when you feel not old enough, strong enough, brave enough, tall enough, or whatever. You might even feel as if everyone is against you. Jesus talked about that with His disciples. He said, "If the world hates you, you know it hated Me before it hated you" (John 15:18). Jesus got left out a lot! Some people didn't believe He was truly God's Son or that He had authority to do the amazing things He did. But Jesus never allowed being left out stop Him. He kept doing what He knew was right, and He didn't let the attitudes of others get in His way. When you feel left out, remember that Jesus understands.

Maybe there are a few activities you aren't very good at—yet! But there are tons of things you do very well. When feeling left out creeps into your thoughts, think about what you're good at. Then talk with Jesus. Just spending time with Him will help you feel better.

*"If the world hates you, you know it
hated Me before it hated you."*
JOHN 15:18

Dear Jesus, whenever I feel left out, I'll remember You know how it feels, and You will help me. . .

I'M SO DiSAPPOiNTED!

Disappointment is one of those uncomfortable feelings you'd rather not have. It lands somewhere between sad and angry. You wanted something. You didn't get it. You wish things had turned out differently, but they didn't, and now you're disappointed. You can't think of anything else but that disappointed feeling filling you up. You're miserable and unhappy, and you don't want to stay that way. So, what can you do to help move that disgusting feeling along?

Sometimes a disappointment can lead you to try something else—to learn a new skill or to put another talent to use. Imagine you tried out for a play, but you didn't get a part. You were so disappointed! The director asked if you would like to be on the stage crew. He said you have amazing art talent, and he thought you would do a great job planning and creating props for the set. But you wanted to be *in* the play! What if you focused instead on your art and how much fun it would be to create the sets? Do you think that might help erase some of your disappointed feelings? There are many things you do well. Maybe this disappointment is a new opportunity to let one of your other skills shine.

When something disappointing happens, it might also help to talk about it. Disappointment is a feeling everyone can relate to. Tell your parents or another adult how you feel. They will understand. They might even have some stories to share about times when they were disappointed and how they got over it. Talking about your feelings helps get them out in the open instead of leaving them stuck inside you swirling around.

When you feel disappointed, go to your quiet place and spend time with Jesus. Remember, Jesus always understands disappointment and every other feeling. Ask Him to help you replace that disappointed feeling with happier feelings and thoughts. Disappointment and other uncomfortable feelings are a part of life. But the good news is those feelings don't last forever! Jesus will give you strength to get over them and move them along.

After you have suffered for awhile, God Himself
will make you perfect. He will keep you in the
right way. He will give you strength.
1 PETER 5:10

Dear Jesus, I feel disappointed. Please help me. . .

DAY 73
LET IT GO

A rule isn't a suggestion. It's a command. God made many rules for us to follow. One of them is today's Bible verse: "Do not seek revenge or bear a grudge against anyone among your people, but love your neighbor as yourself. I am the Lord" (Leviticus 19:18 NIV). When God says, "I am the Lord," it's like He's saying, "Listen. I am the one in charge here." It would be like your mom saying, "Do not disobey me. I am your mother!"

To seek revenge means to get even. When you were little, if your sister scribbled all over your drawing, you might grab the ugliest crayon and scribble all over hers. "There! Take that!" That's revenge. Holding a grudge is not being willing to forgive. When your sister scribbled on your art, you might have said, "I'm never going to speak to you again!" If you never spoke to her again, that would be holding a grudge.

It's not always easy letting go of hurt and anger. Hurt especially likes to hang around inside us. But the longer we hang onto it, the more hurt and angrier we feel. Soon, there's not much room in our hearts for happiness. If we let those feelings hang around too long, we might think the only way to get rid of them is by getting even—and that always turns out badly.

You mess up sometimes, and when you do, you want to be forgiven, right? Maybe you've said something that hurt someone's feelings, but you didn't mean to. When you realize that everyone messes up, it might be easier for you to let go of a grudge and forgive. When you feel hurt or angry, it might also help to talk about it with the other person instead of holding it in.

God says, "Do not seek revenge or bear a grudge against anyone among your people, but love your neighbor as yourself." The loving part can be difficult sometimes, but ask God to help you. He will always lead you in the right way.

"Do not seek revenge or bear a grudge against anyone among your people, but love your neighbor as yourself. I am the LORD."
LEVITICUS 19:18 NIV

Dear God, someone has hurt my feelings. Please help me let go of my angry feelings and do my best to forgive. . .

DAY 74
CREATOR

Have you ever gone hiking? Maybe you hiked woodland trails with your family or a youth group or took a long walk on an ocean beach and picked up shells. If you visited a farm, you might have hiked through fields. Along the way, if you were paying attention, you noticed things that interested you. Maybe you stopped to check them out. When God created the earth, He put little surprises everywhere for you to discover. If you strapped on a backpack and started walking, you couldn't in your lifetime see all the wonderful things God has made. He is the great Creator of the heavens and earth. God never stops creating.

The Bible says God made everything that is seen and things that are not seen. There are places on earth where no human has been. Some places on land are so isolated—tucked away—they are impossible to get to. Some are too cold or too hot to explore. The ocean floor is a vast area with parts that haven't been seen because they are too deep. We can only imagine what's in these places.

You don't have to go far to explore the wonderful things God has made. Look up at the night sky. Check out the moon and stars. The stars you see are only the edge of what's up there that you can't see. There are many more stars beyond your view. Only God knows how many and what extends far beyond them. Tomorrow, take a little walk outside. Look down at the earth. Maybe you will see a weed or flower you hadn't noticed before, or a pretty stone, or a butterfly resting on a flower. God made it all!

Humans have invented some amazing things, but none compare with what God can do. With His great power, He made mountains, oceans, volcanoes, stars, planets. . .and people! God makes people to do His work here on earth and to care for His great creation. In what ways do you think you are doing God's work?

❋

Christ made everything in the heavens and on the earth. He made everything that is seen and things that are not seen. He made all the powers of heaven. Everything was made by Him and for Him.
Colossians 1:16

Dear God, thank You for Your great creations. . .

153

DAY 75
CREATIVE YOU

Today's Bible verse says God made people in His own likeness. What do you think that means? No one knows what God looks like on the outside, but we know from the Bible how God behaves and what He says is right and wrong. God wants us to be a reflection—an image—of His character, of what He is like.

Along with how you behave, you are like God because you create things. God gives you skills and talents that you are good at. You already know some of what you do well, and as you get older, you will discover even more talent that God has tucked away deep inside your hidden heart. Do you enjoy putting colors together to create art? God does too! Look at the color combinations He puts together in nature. You can use His color combinations to inspire your own. Maybe you like to build things. Look at the mountains and rock formations God created. How He put them together might inspire you. Do you make up songs? A new song might be inspired by the birds you hear singing or the rhythm of crickets chirping at night. Or you might be a choreographer, someone who creates new ways to dance. The ways different animals move might provide you with ideas. God has a great imagination. You are like Him in that way too. If you enjoy writing, you can make up short stories, novels, or plays. You can even write instructions to teach others how to create things! God made His people to be creators. In His image, He gives humans the ability to invent. Whether working alone or in groups, people make art, music, stories, dance, buildings, roads, and vehicles. Each day, people come up with amazing new ideas. And who gives them their ideas? The great Creator, God.

Create something today. Use the talent God has given you. Get your girlfriends together and paint a mural or create a dance or a new song. Then share what you make. God shares His creations with everyone on the planet. He wants you to share your creations too.

❊

And God made man in His own likeness. In the likeness of God He made him. He made both male and female.
GENESIS 1:27

Dear God, what would You like me to make today? . . .

BALANCE BEAM

Olympian competitors in gymnastics compete in balance beam events. They do more than just walk on that long wooden beam that's only four inches wide. They run, jump, turn, and do other acrobatics. And they do it all without losing their balance. It takes practice and self-discipline to stay balanced. You need to focus on what you're doing. One step at a time, carefully placed. If you tip too far one way or the other, you lose your balance and fall.

Life is a balancing act. The Bible says there is a time for everything. Think about that: What do you think would happen if you spent all your time doing one thing? Nothing else would get done! But, if you used your time wisely and if you did your best to give the right amount of time to all the important things you needed to do, everything would eventually get done.

Balancing all your activities is tricky sometimes, and that's okay. If you find yourself getting stressed out, maybe you're leaning too much in one direction or trying to do too much at once. Give it a rest. It's perfectly fine to sit down on your imaginary balance beam until you feel ready to get going again. Rest is an important part of keeping your balance in life. Prioritizing things is helpful too. That means putting them in order from most important to least important. Say yes to the most important things, and give yourself permission to say "Later" or "No" to those least important. Just as if you were on a real balance beam, when things begin to feel a little uncomfortable, think carefully about taking that next step. Make it the best step, the right step, to keep your balance.

Remember to communicate with God. He already has a plan for your life. His priorities for you might be different than your own. Begin each day asking God to show you what is important and which things you can say no to or set aside. Imagine every day that you are walking straight ahead on a balance beam and not allowing anything to get in your way.

There is a special time for everything. There is a time for everything that happens under heaven.
ECCLESIASTES 3:1

Dear God, guide me to use my time wisely so I can keep my life in balance. . .

DAY 77
ROLE MODELS

Look in the mirror. Who do you see? Why, it's *you*! It's a girl who's not a little kid anymore. You are growing up, soon to be a teenager. You have so many wonderful and fun things to look forward to. Before long, you will be an adult. A woman! And right now, God is preparing you for that grown-up time in your life. He has put women all around you to be your role models. Mothers, grandmothers, aunts, and other female family members could be your best role models. Teachers will inspire you too. Women who work in careers that interest you, even women who did great things in history can be role models. If you pay attention to the godly things they do and if you follow their examples, they will help guide you in the right direction.

What are role models good for? They are great encouragers. If you think you can't, these women know that you can. They've faced obstacles in life like the ones you face now, and they discovered that when they thought they couldn't—they could! Along the way, they learned to be patient and not give up. Your role models have messed up sometimes. They know what it feels like not to succeed the first time and to try again. And godly role models know that sometimes they've allowed sin to creep into their lives. They've done things they wish they hadn't. A godly woman knows to take responsibility for her actions and to ask for forgiveness. She understands that no matter how badly she messed up, God will forgive her all the time. Role models are there to comfort you when you fall and to help you grow up. They help prepare you for the future.

Think about the godly women in your life, those who know God, love Him, and do their best to please Him. Which of these women do you think is your best role model? Why do you think so? What have you learned from her so far? You've just answered three questions about your best role model. Now, think of three questions you would like to ask her.

She makes herself ready with strength,
and makes her arms strong.
PROVERBS 31:17

Dear God, lead me to godly women who will give me good advice not just now but throughout my life. . .

BOYS AND DATING

One of the Bible's mysteries is who really wrote chapter thirty-one in the book of Proverbs. The Bible says it was written by King Lemuel of Massa. But no one knows if this king really existed. The Bible says nothing more about him, and he's not listed in the history of God's people, the Israelites. Some think Proverbs 31 was written by King Solomon—the wise king who wrote many of the other proverbs. Whoever wrote this chapter, he was thinking of good advice he received from his mom. The chapter begins, "[These are] the words of Lemuel king of Massa, which his mother taught him" (Proverbs 31:1). The king goes on to share what his mom told him about the qualities he should look for in a wife. The king's mother wanted him to marry a godly woman. She told him that finding a wife who was beautiful on the outside wasn't as important as finding one whose hidden heart belonged to God.

When you are a little older and begin dating, maybe your mom will give you wise advice and tell you to focus on what's in a boy's heart instead of how he looks. What kind of man would you like to marry one day? Can you think of several qualities—good things—you would look for in a husband? You might say you would want him to be kind and someone who cares about others. Maybe strong and brave. A man who works hard to provide for his family's needs. Someone who is loyal, honest, and faithful to both you and to God, a good dad, a man who loves you. . . When you look for boys to date, look for some of those good qualities. Dating godly boys will lead you one day to the godly man you will marry.

King Lemuel's mom gave him good advice about finding a godly wife. Maybe you have heard your pastor talk about the Proverbs 31 woman. She is a woman who loves God, a woman with good qualities, the kind of woman and wife you want to become one day.

Who can find a good wife? For she is worth far more than rubies that make one rich.
PROVERBS 31:10

Dear God, help me to build on those qualities that will help me become a godly woman. . .

EARLY RISER

What gets you up on time in the morning? Are you someone who jumps joyfully out of bed, or does your mom have to shout, "Get up!" Maybe after shouting a few times, she needs to come into your room and make sure you get out of bed.

Proverbs 31 talks about early risers. When King Lemuel's mom told him what to look for in a wife, she said to look for someone willing to get up early to care for her family and help them start the day. Maybe your mom is an early riser. If you wake up before your alarm goes off, you might hear your mom doing chores. She could be making breakfast for you and your siblings or preparing a bag lunch for you to take to school. Do you hear the dishwasher or washing machine running? Mom might be trying to get a few things done in the early morning before her day gets even busier. Getting up early is part of what wives and moms do to help care for their families. And moms aren't the only early risers. Dads are too! At your house, maybe it's Dad who wakes you up, makes your breakfast, and does the laundry before the sun comes up.

Getting an early start on your day is a good and godly thing. Early morning is also a good time to talk with God without being interrupted. Talking to Him first thing in the morning reminds you to focus on Him throughout your day. When you get up early, you know you will have plenty of time to get dressed, your backpack in order, and to the school bus on time. If you allow yourself a few extra minutes in the morning, you are less likely to leave your lunch on the kitchen counter or forget to tuck your homework into your backpack before you leave for school.

Give it a try. Get up fifteen minutes early tomorrow morning. Check out what your parents are doing when you get up, and tell them thanks for being there to care for you and help you start your day.

She rises while it is still night and makes
food for all those in her house.
PROVERBS 31:15

Dear God, every morning when the alarm sounds, I will get up without being told. . .

MARTHA

The Bible tells about two sisters, Mary and Martha. They and their brother, Lazarus, were dear friends of Jesus. When Jesus came to town, Mary and Martha cared for Him in their home.

One day when Jesus was visiting them, Martha got busy making supper. She was working hard all by herself preparing the food. At the same time, Mary was sitting with Jesus listening to everything He said. Martha came to Jesus. "Do You see that my sister is not helping me? Tell her to help me." Jesus said to her, "Martha, Martha, you are worried and troubled about many things. Only a few things are important, even just one. Mary has chosen the good thing. It will not be taken away from her" (Luke 10:40–42). Jesus knew that while working hard is a good quality for a godly woman, she needs to remember that God comes first. He is more important than anything.

A time came when Jesus tested the sisters' faith in Him. Their brother, Lazarus, got very sick while Jesus was out of town. Mary and Martha sent for Jesus because they knew He could heal Lazarus. But Jesus didn't come. Lazarus died. Several days later, Jesus arrived there, and Martha went to meet Him. She said to Jesus, "Lord, if You had been here, my brother would not have died. I know even now God will give You whatever You ask" (John 11:21–22). Martha's faith in Jesus was strong. Even after Lazarus died, she believed Jesus had the power to raise him from the dead. She knew Jesus had control over the future of everyone and everything. Jesus did bring

Lazarus back to life, and Martha was filled with joy. Martha was a Proverbs 31 kind of woman. She was strong and hardworking at home caring for her family, but she was also strong in her faith. She honored Jesus, and because she knew Jesus could do anything, Martha had a positive attitude about the future.

Do you know someone like her?

Her clothes are strength and honor. She is full of joy about the future. . . . She looks well to the ways of those in her house, and does not eat the bread of doing nothing.
PROVERBS 31:25, 27

Dear God, help me to become a hardworking woman who has a strong faith like Martha's. . .

WISDOM AND KINDNESS

When you were little, you asked tons of questions: "Do people grow tails?" "When we go on vacation, can we go to the moon?" "Mom, were you ever a baby?" Now that you're older, those questions sound silly. The questions you ask today are about more important things. "Why do people get sick and die?" "Why is that person homeless?" "Mom, why can't I stay up as late as you?" It's good to ask questions and know there are godly women who will listen and help you figure things out.

Proverbs 31 says a godly woman speaks with wisdom. When you wonder about things, which women in your life can you go to for wise advice? Moms, grandmothers, and aunts are great choices. So are godly teachers and counselors. They know you need sound answers to your questions, and they are willing to help. These trustworthy women are always there for you. It's their purpose to answer your questions and guide you so one day you will become a wise woman too.

Along with saying a godly woman is wise, Proverbs 31 adds that "the teaching of kindness is on her tongue" (Proverbs 31:26). If you ask a Proverbs 31 woman a question, she will never make you feel foolish for asking. She will treat you with kindness. Through the example she sets, you will learn kindness too.

Remember, you are a Proverbs 31 woman in training, and you can use some of what you've already learned. If your little sister asks you, "Do dolls die?" will you say, "No," and move on, or will you take time to find out why she asked? Finding out the why behind her question shows you care. When you learn what caused her to ask, you can give a wise answer. Your little sister might notice too how kind you were to listen and give her some of your time.

Read all of Proverbs 31 in your Bible. Women who lived in Old Testament days did different kinds of work than most women today, but still they had many of the same godly qualities—working hard, caring for their families, giving wise advice, and being kind.

❋

She opens her mouth with wisdom. The teaching of kindness is on her tongue.
Proverbs 31:26

Dear God, lead me to become a woman who is kind and wise. . .

MARY, JESUS' MOM

Mary, the mother of Jesus, didn't just fit the definition of a Proverbs 31 woman. She was the one woman out of all those on earth whom God chose to give birth to His Son. The Bible says when God sent an angel to tell Mary the news, she knew people might gossip about her. She was going to have a baby, and she wasn't yet married. Still, she trusted in God's plan. Mary told the angel, "I am willing to be used of the Lord. Let it happen to me as you have said" (Luke 1:38). She faithfully accepted what God wanted her to do.

Mary was engaged to a good man named Joseph, and he accepted God's plan too. They were married and traveled to Joseph's hometown for the census—an official count of the people who lived there. The journey was rough, and when they arrived, all the rooms to rent were taken. Jesus was born in a place where the animals lived. Instead of a crib, Mary lay baby Jesus in a manger, a long hay-filled feeding box for the animals. Mary was a strong, Proverbs 31 kind of woman who made do with what she had.

We can imagine it wasn't easy for Mary, knowing she was chosen to raise God's Son. It was an overwhelming responsibility for a young woman. The Bible says very little about Jesus' childhood, but we can guess that Mary raised Him well. God knew she would be the godliest kind of mom to guide His Son to manhood. We can imagine that Mary was a wonderful mother and that she taught her children (there were others in addition to Jesus) to love, honor, and obey God.

In Proverbs 31, when the king shared what his mother told him about finding a godly wife, she said, "Look for a woman whose children and husband will honor her and say to her, 'Well done.' " That's the kind of woman Mary was—as close to God as any woman on earth could be.

Her children rise up and honor her. Her husband does also, and he praises her, saying: "Many daughters have done well, but you have done better than all of them."
PROVERBS 31:28–29

Dear God, thank You for Bible stories
about godly women like Mary. . .

SUDDEN CHANGES

How do you feel about change? Your new hairstyle is a change that you love. When Mom allowed you to add a little purple streak to it, that was a change you adored! Maybe you've decided to change the way you dress. You ditched solid bright colors for patterns that express who you are. Change is fun when you can control what changes. But what about those changes you can't control?

Some turnarounds are unexpected. A new job for a parent can lead to a big move. A shift to a new school means new teachers and making new friends. An illness or broken bone is a change that can keep you from doing the things you love. When a change happens suddenly, it can feel like everything is different. You might feel sad, scared, worried, or even lost. That's when it's time to turn to God.

The Bible says, "We know that God makes all things work together for the good of those who love Him and are chosen to be a part of His plan" (Romans 8:28). God can change any situation, but sometimes He allows unexpected changes to change us. Your parent's job change and that big move to a new place and new school might lead you to the best friend you will ever have, a lifelong friend. That illness or broken bone could open your eyes to caregiving and guide you toward becoming a doctor, nurse, or paramedic one day. Whatever happens, God sees. He knows. Every change is part of His big plan for you and your future.

Today's Bible verse is God speaking to you. He says He will do new things in your life. Those changes could make you feel lonely, like you are walking all by yourself through a desert. But God says He will work things out according to His plan. He will help you find a road out of that imaginary desert, and instead of seeing only sand, He will open your eyes to see something new and good.

"See, I will do a new thing. It will begin happening now. Will you not know about it? I will even make a road in the wilderness, and rivers in the desert."
ISAIAH 43:19

Dear God, when things suddenly change, I trust You to guide me toward something new and good. . .

GOD DOESN'T CHANGE

Pop quiz. Think fast! Name three things that have changed in the past twenty-four hours. Maybe you thought of everyday things like the weather, the news, or your feelings. Maybe you experienced a bigger change—you had a birthday and now you are a year older, or your mom had a baby and instead of two siblings you have three. Everything changes. Some changes are small, others are big. Some happen quickly, others happen little by little over a period of years. There is only one thing that will never change. God! He is the same today as He was yesterday. He is the same as He has been forever. God and everything about Him will never change.

God has no beginning and no end. He has been God forever. He is all powerful. There is nothing He cannot do; everything God does comes easy for Him. He doesn't have to work to make something happen. With His thoughts and words, He can command anything to obey Him. God never sleeps. He is everywhere all the time. And God knows everything all the time from the tiniest things like how many hairs are on your head right now to big things like how long the earth will exist and what will happen when it ends. God is wise. He never has to think about how to solve a problem. His wisdom is perfect. God rules heaven and earth. He keeps all His promises. He never lies. He is always good and fair. God is kind. He gives us more than we deserve, and He is quick to forgive us when we mess up and ask for His forgiveness. God is holy—perfectly good in a perfect way. No human or any false made-up god is equal to the one true, holy God. He is the great Creator. He made you, and He will love you and be faithful and loyal to you forever. Jesus and the Holy Spirit are both parts of God, and they don't change either.

You can always trust God to be with you and help you through all the changes that happen in your life. His perfect love for you has no beginning and no end.

"For I, the Lord, do not change."
MALACHI 3:6

Dear God, when everything around me
changes, You will never change. . .

THE NAMES OF GOD

A name is a personal and special thing. When you were born, your parents thought a lot about what to name you. Along with your given name, Mom and Dad might call you names that remind you of how much you are loved, names like honey, dear, and sweetheart. Do you have a nickname? Maybe a shortened version of your name? Your friends might call you Ally instead of Allison. Or maybe you like to laugh, so your grandpa calls you Giggles. Silly nicknames like that can stick around for a while in a family. Grandpa might still call you Giggles when you are twenty-five!

Did you know God has more than one name? When His people, the Israelites, were slaves in Egypt, God told Moses, "Go to Pharaoh and say to him, 'The Lord, the God of the Hebrews, says this: "Let My people go" ' " (Exodus 9:1).

Then Moses said to God, "Suppose I go to the People of Israel and I tell them, 'The God of your fathers sent me to you'; and they ask me, 'What is his name?' What do I tell them?" God said to Moses, "I-AM-WHO-I-AM. Tell the People of Israel, 'I-AM sent me to you. . . . GOD, the God of your fathers, the God of Abraham, the God of Isaac, and the God of Jacob sent me to you.' This has always been my name, and this is how I always will be known (Exodus 3:13–15 MSG).

I AM is just one of God's many names. He is also known as our heavenly Father, friend, and the comforter. Some people call Him "El Shaddai," which means God almighty, or "Yahweh," which means Holy God of Israel. God and Jesus are the same person, so Jesus and His other names, Christ and Savior, are also names for God. Jesus is also known as Lord, the Prince of Peace, and the Messiah.

This one God, known by many different names, knows your name! And whatever you choose to call Him, He hears you when you say His name, and He loves to hear you pray.

"They will call on My name, and I will answer them. I will say, 'They are My people,' and they will say, 'The Lord is my God.' "
ZECHARIAH 13:9

Dear God, You are my heavenly
Father and my friend. . .

FREEDOM

Do you wish you had more freedom? Most kids do. They want to get rid of the rules, have exciting adventures, and try new things. Wanting more freedom is part of growing up. When you finally become a grown-up, you will be free. You won't have Mom and Dad or anyone else telling you, "You can't." You will be responsible for yourself and your choices. Sounds good, doesn't it?

From the beginning, God has given people freedom to make their own choices. He makes the rules, but He lets people choose whether to follow them. In the Garden of Eden, Adam and Eve had freedom to choose. They made a poor choice when they decided to follow Satan's suggestion instead of God's rule not to eat fruit from one certain tree. In fact, that first poor choice allowed evil to enter God's perfect world.

Freedom is all about making choices. Too often, people choose to follow Satan instead of God. A poor choice leads to sin, and there are consequences. Until Jesus came, sin made it difficult for a person's hidden heart to be pure enough for heaven. But Jesus changed that. When He died on the cross for the punishment sin deserved, He made our hearts pure and clean. That doesn't mean, though, that His death stopped people from making poor choices. They were still free to sin. What changed was that even when people used their freedom to sin, there was a way for them to get to heaven.

In a letter to his friends, Jesus' follower Paul wrote about freedom. He reminded his friends that although they were free to do whatever they wanted, they should be careful not to use their freedom to sin. Paul's advice wasn't just for his friends. It is in the Bible because God wants us to use our freedom to please Him.

When your parents allow you more freedom, remember to make wise choices. Enjoy your freedom and have fun, but don't use your freedom to follow Satan into sin. When you practice making wise choices now, it will be easier to choose wisely when you are all grown up.

You were chosen to be free. Be careful that you do not please your old selves by sinning because you are free.
GALATIANS 5:13

Dear Lord, help me to use my freedom to please You. . .

SERIOUSLY?

When you were little, your older brother might have said outrageous things to scare you (older brothers can be naughty that way). If he said there was a hungry tyrannosaurus rex hiding under your bed, you probably believed him. Even after your parents calmed you down and gave your brother a time-out, you might have still been afraid of that hungry dinosaur. But you are older now. If your brother said, "Hey, there's a tyrannosaurus rex under your bed ready to eat you," you would roll your eyes, shoot him a bored look, and say, "Seriously?" You've learned discernment—the ability to judge wisely and decide whether something is the truth or a lie.

Some ideas are so "out there" that it's easy to know they're untrue. Others, though, are carefully disguised by Satan. He can make a lie sound like the truth and make something evil look good. Think about him in the Garden of Eden persuading Eve to taste the fruit on God's forbidden tree. "Come on," he said. "Try it. It's good." The fruit did look good to Eve. Satan's well-chosen words convinced her that eating it would not displease God. So, she took a bite, and the rest is history. Did Eve mean to let sin loose into the world? No. But she got caught in Satan's trap.

As you learn about God and His rules, you are better able to tell when Satan is trying to trick you. The Bible says not to believe every spirit. Satan is a spirit. He doesn't have a human body. He is invisible like God. But Satan is not like God in any other way. Instead of leading you toward what's good, right, and pure, Satan will always lead you away from God and into sin.

If you're uncertain whether something is right or wrong, test it. Is it something Jesus would do? Is it something that will please God? If you're still unsure, don't act on it. Instead, spend time with God in prayer. Ask Him to lead you in the right direction.

Dear Christian friends, do not believe every spirit. But test the spirits to see if they are from God for there are many false preachers in the world.
1 JOHN 4:1

Dear heavenly Father, please help me to discern good from evil so I won't sin. . .

DAY 88
BE REAL

Something that is a copy or in disguise can be used to fool people into thinking that it's real. For example, a sparkly toy ring you bought at a dollar store is a reproduction of an expensive ring you would buy at a jewelry shop. It's pretty, but it isn't real. It's fake. If you wore a costume and mask to a dress-up party, you would still be the real you underneath. But with a great disguise, even your friends wouldn't know it's you.

Do you know a girl who copies the behavior of someone she admires? Maybe she talks and dresses like that person. She likes the same music, videos, and dances. She wants the same friends. She wants so much to be like that person she disguises who she really is. She trades a fake copy of herself for the one-of-a-kind special girl God created her to be. That girl has hidden her real self from the world. Instead of allowing her personality to shine brightly, like a real diamond ring, she's settled for less.

Jesus told His followers, "Let your light shine before others." He didn't make us to be a copy of someone else. He made each of us special. He created you just as you are, and He wants the whole world to know the real you. Jesus said, "Let your light shine before others, that they may see your good deeds and glorify your Father in heaven" (Matthew 5:16 NIV). He meant, let everyone know that God is the only one you are trying to please. Do what God says is good, right, and true, and be a role model for others.

If you find yourself wanting to copy a person's behavior and words, think more about pleasing God than being popular or accepted. Paul told his friends: "Each person should judge his own actions and not compare himself with others" (Galatians 6:4 NCV). Be real. Be the girl God made you to be.

✳

Do you think I am trying to make people accept me? No, God is the One I am trying to please. Am I trying to please people? If I still wanted to please people, I would not be a servant of Christ.
GALATIANS 1:10 NCV

Dear Jesus, I will be the real me. I'll let my light shine for the whole world to see. . .

SELF-TALK

How would you describe yourself to others? What would you say about your looks? What would you tell them about your personality? Would you share with them how you *really* feel about what you look like and who you are?

In our thoughts, we are always judging ourselves and our actions. There are two voices speaking to us inside our hearts. One, the Holy Spirit, tells us the truth about ourselves and leads us toward God. The other, Satan, tells lies. He leads us away from God. If you think to yourself, *I look nice today*, who do you think set that thought inside your head? If, instead, you think, *My hair looks weird, my nose is too big, and I look like a gerbil,* where do you think that thought came from? Satan is always competing with the Holy Spirit. He is in a battle to take over your thoughts. It's up to you to decide who wins.

Self-talk is what we think about ourselves. Those thoughts can be positive or negative. That wise king, Solomon, wrote in Proverbs, "Be careful what you think, because your thoughts run your life" (Proverbs 4:23 NCV). If you believe all those negative thoughts Satan puts inside your head, you will think you aren't worth very much. But if you believe what the Holy Spirit says about you, then you will know who you really are—the daughter of the King of all kings. You are God's child!

I'm not good enough is a negative thought. Turn it around. Tell yourself, "I *am* good enough! The Bible says, 'I can do all things because Christ gives me strength' " (Philippians 4:13). A sure way to chase Satan's thoughts out of your head is to fire back with a Bible verse. He hates that! If Satan says anything at all about the way you look, tell him that God made you in His image (Genesis 1:27). God made you beautiful inside and out. So take that, Satan!

The Holy Spirit will always guide your thoughts toward God and pleasing Him. He will help you feel good about how you look on the outside and who you are on the inside.

Be careful what you think, because
your thoughts run your life.
PROVERBS 4:23 NCV

Dear God, help me to listen to the Holy Spirit
when He speaks inside my heart. . .

DAY 90
STAND UP

You know who you are. You are God's girl! You are learning right from wrong according to what the Bible and the Holy Spirit say. You mess up sometimes, but you know God forgives you. Every day, you do your best to behave in ways that please Him. You know what God expects from you, but there are those around you who don't know God. They have no respect for Him and His rules. You might find that upsetting. So, what should you do?

God wants you to stand up for what you know is right. He wants you to set a godly example for others. But there is a right way to stand up for what you believe in. Do you remember what Ecclesiastes 3:1 says: "There is a special time for everything"? Ecclesiastes also says, "There is. . .a time to be quiet and a time to speak" (Ecclesiastes 3:7). If you saw someone behaving in a way God wouldn't approve of, would you stand up and shout, "God sees what you are doing! Stop it! You are behaving badly!" No, you probably would not. What could you do instead? First, set a good example by not going along with the bad behavior. Then, if you know that person well enough, a sibling for example or your best friend, you might say privately that you didn't appreciate the bad behavior because you knew God wouldn't like it.

It takes courage to stand up for what you believe in. It takes courage to stand up for someone who you know is being mistreated or to say "no" when everyone else is saying "yes."

Sometimes standing up for what you believe can be as simple as just walking away. Other times, it means speaking up. If you do speak up, then speak with kindness. Always tell the truth. Don't use ugly, mean, or hateful words or try to embarrass the other person. If you feel it's not safe to speak up against something you know is wrong, find an adult to help. If you aren't sure what to do, ask God. The Holy Spirit will guide you.

But we are to hold to the truth with love in our hearts.
EPHESIANS 4:15

Dear God, teach me the best ways to stand up for what I believe in and for what I know is right. . .

DREAMS

God is planting seeds of big hopes and dreams in your heart. He has your whole life planned, and He wants it filled with wonderful experiences. What are you dreaming about today? Maybe your sister is in a drill team that marches in parades. It's your dream to do that too. You tell yourself, "When I'm old enough to join the team, that's what I want to do!" Or maybe while you're doing your homework at the kitchen table, you hear someone in the apartment downstairs playing the guitar, and you think, *I want to do that*! What others do can get us dreaming about what we might enjoy. All day, little dreams float in and out of our thoughts.

Sometimes, a little dream starts to grow. You find yourself thinking about it more often. It could be a physical goal, like becoming the best in gymnastics or dance. It might be an academic—educational—goal, like entering a spelling bee, science fair, or winning an essay contest. A goal can be a personality change too, like becoming more caring and aware of the needs of others or being more grateful for what you have. When little dreams become bigger dreams, follow them! See where they lead.

In Joseph's Bible story, we learn that when he was a teen, God gave him some real dreams to think about. While sleeping, Joseph had two dreams that made him believe God had something great planned for him. In those dreams, Joseph saw bundles of grain and the sun, moon, and stars bowing down to him. When he told his family about the dreams, his brothers made fun of him. They called him "the dreamer." But God did have great plans for Joseph. When he grew up, Joseph became governor of Egypt. When people came to see him, they bowed as a way of showing him respect. Sometimes, God gives us little hints about our future, as He did Joseph.

If you find a dream often coming into your thoughts, talk with God about it. Ask Him to guide you. If it is God's will for you to follow that dream, ask Him to make it grow.

❋

*May He give you the desire of your heart,
and make all your plans go well.*
PSALM 20:4

Dear God, if that dream was from
You, please make it grow. . .

CELEBRATE!

Even way back in Bible times, people enjoyed celebrations. Much like the parties and festivals we have today, people ate, danced, and had fun. Passover was one of the first holidays people celebrated during Old Testament times. Many still celebrate it today. Passover honors when God led His people out of slavery in Egypt and punished those who held them as slaves. In the New Testament, we read that Jesus celebrated Passover. Just before He was arrested, He and His disciples shared a special dinner to celebrate the holiday. Jesus attended other kinds of celebrations too. The Bible says that He, His mother, and His disciples went to a wedding celebration in a village called Cana (John 2).

Holidays and special days have always been in God's plan for His people. He wants us to be joyful and have fun. Do you have a favorite holiday? Christmas and Easter are holidays that celebrate Jesus. Christmas celebrates His birthday and Easter honors the day Jesus arose from the dead three days after He died on the cross. Along with Easter and Christmas, we celebrate other holidays and special days: birthdays, weddings, graduations, the last day of school, a great report card, a recital, receiving an honor or award. We get together to celebrate with family and friends at fairs, festivals, parades, and picnics. We celebrate with fireworks, special foods, decorations, games, dances, and all kinds of fun.

God wants us to be joyful. He wants us to get together and play. He also wants us to celebrate Him and His awesomeness! How can you celebrate God? By being thankful for all He is and all He does, by praising Him, singing worship songs, and by telling others how wonderful He is.

Celebrate something today. It doesn't have to be anything big, like a birthday or holiday. Think about some way God has blessed you, and then do something special to celebrate. Sing to the Lord. Dance. Eat ice cream! Celebrate being alive and the wonderful life God has given you.

❈

Then all the people went away to eat and drink, to send some of their food to others, and to celebrate with great joy.
NEHEMIAH 8:12 NCV

Dear God, today I will celebrate You! I will remember with joyfulness all You have done for me and how great You are. . .

THANKSGIVING

Each November, Americans celebrate the holiday called "Thanksgiving." It is a tradition that goes all the way back to a festival in the autumn of 1621 in Plymouth, Massachusetts. The pilgrims—a group of travelers who had sailed from England to America in 1620—had worked hard to make their new land a safe and comfortable place to live. They learned from the Native Americans, who lived nearby, how to grow and harvest food. The first Thanksgiving was a feast celebrating God's gift of a bountiful harvest. The pilgrims and their Native American friends got together for a festival that lasted three days. There was plenty of food to share. One of the pilgrims, Edward Winslow, wrote in his journal, "By the goodness of God, we are so far from want."

It wasn't until 1863 that Thanksgiving was celebrated in America as it is today, every year on the fourth Thursday of November. It came as an official announcement from President Abraham Lincoln. He said, "I. . .invite my fellow-citizens in every part of the United States, and also those who are at sea and those who are (traveling) in foreign lands, to set apart and observe the last Thursday of November. . .as a Day of Thanksgiving and Praise to our (generous) Father who dwelleth in the heavens."

Every year since, Americans have gathered on Thanksgiving Day to praise God for His many blessings. How does your family celebrate Thanksgiving? Do you attend church on or near the holiday to give thanks to God? Maybe you sing hymns and songs of thanks and praise in your church service. In some homes, before a family eats their Thanksgiving meal, they each say something they are thankful for.

Thanksgiving is a special day we set aside to give thanks to God. But we should be thankful to Him every day, not just for a year's worth of blessings, but for all the blessings we receive each day.

When spending time in prayer, remember to say, "Thank You." Get in the habit of beginning your bedtime prayer with thanksgiving. Share with God a long list of things you are grateful for.

*I will praise God's name in song and
glorify him with thanksgiving.*
PSALM 69:30 NIV

Dear God, I have so many wonderful things to be grateful for. You have blessed me in so many ways. . .

THANK YOU, JESUS!

Imagine your basketball team just won the championship. You and the other girls clap and jump up and down with happiness. You hug each other and share congratulations. The team worked hard to get to this competition, and you won! In the middle of the celebration, your coach reminds you to shake hands with members of the losing team and thank them for a great game. Then you hurry home to tell your family and friends the good news. What a great day! But something is missing. Can you guess what it is?

In Luke 17:11–19, the Bible tells that while Jesus walked to a place called Jerusalem, ten men with a contagious skin disease called out to Him. "Jesus. . .take pity on us!" (v. 13) They knew Jesus had healed others, and they wanted to be healed too. But instead of simply agreeing to heal the men, Jesus said, "Go and show yourselves to the religious leaders" (v. 14). The men had faith in and trusted Jesus, so they obeyed Him. While on their way, they were suddenly healed! Can you imagine the celebration? They might have been jumping for joy, like your basketball team did. The men ran off to tell their family and friends, "Come, celebrate with us! We were healed!" But one man turned back. He went to Jesus, bowed down at His feet, and thanked Him. Jesus asked, "Were there not ten men who were healed? Where are the other nine?" (v. 17) The other men had been so happy celebrating, they forgot to thank the one who had healed them. They had forgotten that if it weren't for Jesus, they wouldn't have been healed.

Jesus is what was missing from the celebration after your basketball game. No one remembered to thank Him. Jesus was responsible for bringing your team members together and helping you to become strong and play well. Jesus made it possible for you to win the game. He deserves the thanks. It's easy to get caught up in a celebration and forget to include Jesus. But try to remember to come back to say, "Thank You, Jesus."

❋

One of them turned back when he saw he was healed. He thanked God with a loud voice.
LUKE 17:15

Dear Jesus, thank You for making this great day happen! Let's You and I celebrate together. . .

ELIJAH AND THE CHARIOT

In the Bible, in 1 Kings 18, there is a story about Elijah, one of God's prophets—a man God chose to speak for Him and guide His people. An evil king, Ahab, ruled the land from the capital city, Jezreel. Ahab and most of his kingdom worshipped false gods, so God decided to punish them. God sent Elijah to tell the king there would be no rain on his land for three years. Everything in Ahab's kingdom dried up. But God sent Elijah to a safe place where he had plenty of food and water. During those three years, Elijah, with God's help, convinced the people in Ahab's kingdom to stop worshipping false gods. When the people turned to the real God, Elijah knew God would send rain. He told Ahab he'd better get in his chariot and safely home because a huge rainstorm was coming. The strong horses pulling King Ahab's chariot made it go very fast. But God had one more surprise for the evil king. While Ahab's chariot raced to Jezreel, the king saw Elijah running alongside. Elijah outran the chariot and arrived in Jezreel before the king. It was God's way of showing His power to King Ahab. That a man could outrun a chariot was a miracle. But God gave Elijah supernatural strength to do it.

Sometimes, God gives people a power boost to win competitions and do other amazing things. When you want strength like Elijah's, ask God and allow Him to lead you one step at a time. Like Elijah, trust in God's power and believe He can help you do anything. Spend time in prayer talking with Him and listening to His instructions. When you trust God with a faith like Elijah's, He will lead you to do your best at whatever you try. With God's help, you will accomplish many goals in your life. Maybe some with supernatural strength. But, while focusing on your goals, focus more on God. Work as if you are working for Him. If you think you can't keep going, ask God to provide you with His power. Then, put your faith and trust in Him.

❈

He gives strength to the weak. And He gives
power to him who has little strength.
ISAIAH 40:29

Dear God, please help me to keep
going. I need a power boost. . .

DAY 96
SLEEP

"Dad, read me a story." At bedtime when you were little, you probably asked your dad or mom to read to you before you went to sleep. Listening to your parent's gentle voice helped you relax. In the Bible, we learn that when King Ahasuerus (Esther 1–10) had trouble sleeping, he commanded his servants to read him the records of the kingdom. It was sort of a journal of everything the king had done during his reign. Can you imagine how boring that must have been? For sure, it put the king to sleep.

Maybe you have trouble sleeping sometimes. It's not unusual. Most kids and grown-ups have nights when they lay down in bed with their eyes wide open and thoughts racing through their heads. Worry can keep you awake. On the night before the first day of a new school year, many kids feel anxious and can't sleep. Waiting for news about something important or someone you care about can keep you awake too. And if you don't like storms, thunder and lightning might keep you tossing and turning in your bed. Changing time in the spring and fall can mess with your sleep. So can staying in an unfamiliar place while on vacation or anything that changes your normal bedtime schedule. There are many different reasons for not sleeping. Sometimes, there doesn't seem to be any reason at all.

Reading before bedtime might help you relax. So can putting away any electronics an hour before bedtime. If you can't shut off those anxious thoughts racing through your head, try turning them around by remembering what Paul told his friends: "Keep. . .thinking about whatever is true, whatever is respected, whatever is right, whatever is pure, whatever can be loved, and whatever is well thought of. If there is anything good and worth giving thanks for, think about these things" (Philippians 4:8). Turn your thoughts toward God and His blessings. And remember, God never sleeps. Every night He is there next to your bed watching over you. So, give all your worries and thoughts to Him, and get some rest.

✿

I will lie down and sleep in peace.
O Lord, You alone keep me safe.
PSALM 4:8

Dear God, I'm having trouble sleeping tonight.
Please take my thoughts and worries for
a while so I can get some sleep. . .

197

LIVING IN AN ELECTRONIC WORLD

Computers, tablets, smartphones, video games, earphones, smart televisions, and smart speakers. We live in a world where electronics and technology are all around us.

The world wasn't always filled with electronic gadgets. In Bible times, none of these things existed. The world was a much quieter and less complicated place. People walked instead of riding in cars, they wrote letters instead of texting. If they wanted to hear music, they sang or played instruments. Phones didn't exist and wouldn't for a very long time. Can you imagine Jesus and His disciples walking along looking down at their smartphones! When the Bible was written, people couldn't begin to imagine the world we live in today.

Technology is a good thing because it connects God's people all around the world. We can video chat with a friend in another country, and although we speak different languages, electronic devices can translate our words so we understand each other. And how could we live without our smartphones? You probably have one so you can connect with your parents wherever you go. Technology brings us videos, music, games, and fun. But too much technology can be a distraction. It can lead us away from God and what He says is important.

Paul wrote to his friends, "I am allowed to do all things, but not everything is good for me to do! Even if I am free to do all things, I will not do them if I think it would be hard for me to stop when I know I should" (1 Corinthians 6:12). His is good advice for today. We can become so dependent on devices that it's almost impossible to put them down even when we know we should. If that happens, our thoughts and eyes are on the world instead of focused on God.

Which would you put first, spending time playing video games and texting with your friends or spending time with God? Try this: don't use your tablet and smartphone or play video games for one whole day. See if you can do it.

❊

Do not love the world or anything in the world. If anyone loves the world, the Father's love is not in him.
1 JOHN 2:15

Dear God, help me never to allow spending time with my electronics to become more important than spending time with You. . .

WHERE IN THE WORLD?

Where in the world would you like to go? Your first thought might be to someplace you enjoy—a theme park, the beach, or to visit a relative or friend. But what about someplace far away, across the ocean, to a country on the other side of the world?

God's world is a big, beautiful, and amazing place. It is made up of all kinds of people speaking different languages and living in different ways. Some live in big cities, others in small towns, and some in villages tucked away in places where few visitors go. God often sends His missionaries to those places to bring people food, clothing, and medicine. He sends them to teach language, reading, writing, and math. Even more important, He sends them to share the good news about Jesus. That's what missionaries do—they lead others to Jesus.

Some missionaries spend their entire lives in a foreign country. But many others do mission work volunteering for short Christian mission trips set by their churches. They help communities near and far by building and repairing houses, cleaning up after storms, and providing food, clothing, and supplies to people in need. They help special needs kids and volunteer at charity events that raise money for good causes. Maybe you have joined with your church youth group to do some mission work in your own community.

When you grow up, your job might take you away from where you live right now, or when you marry your Prince Charming, you might move away with him to a different city or state. You can't know where God will send you, but He knows. And wherever you go, God wants you to serve Him by helping others and telling them about Jesus.

Now answer this question again, this time thinking about how you would like to serve others when you grow up: where in the world would you like to go? Maybe someday God will send you to do His work on the other side of the world.

"Go and make followers of all the nations. . . . Teach them to do all the things I have told you. And I am with you always, even to the end of the world."
MATTHEW 28:19–20

Dear God, I wonder where You will send me? Wherever I go, I want to serve You and help others.

IF I GET LOST

Have you ever walked through a corn maze? Corn mazes are a popular and fun activity in the fall, but while it might be easy to solve a maze on paper, it's difficult when you are actually inside a maze. You can't see what is ahead of you. Sometimes, you need to decide to turn left or right. If you choose wrong, you find yourself going in circles or at a dead end. Some mazes are so huge, you can even get lost. If you can't find your way out, you could have to call for help. It's a good idea to have a plan. A map will help you get through the maze. Jotting down the number of someone outside the maze who can help is a good idea too. And, of course, that means being prepared and having your phone with you and charged.

Life can be a lot like a corn maze. It has a beginning and an end, twists and turns, and choices to make about whether to go this way or that. A wrong choice means having to find your way back, and that's not always easy. It's a good idea to be prepared and think before you act. Sometimes, though, no matter how well prepared you are, you'll still choose wrong. You will find yourself lost and needing help. When that happens, there is someone you can call on—Jesus! He knows where you are, and He will help you find your way back.

Jesus is the best first responder. As soon as He hears your call, He will find you. He's ready and able to save you from whatever sin got you into trouble. You don't have to do anything other than say, "Jesus, I messed up. Please help me." You don't have to worry that He will punish you for getting lost. Instead, He will get you back on the right path. Jesus will go ahead of you and guide you all the days of your life. And when you get to the end of your life, Jesus will lead you straight into heaven.

✳

"For the Son of Man came to look for and to save from the punishment of sin those who are lost."
LUKE 19:10

Dear Jesus, You are my best friend and Savior. Guide me through the maze of my life. . .

ALIVE FOREVER

When God created you, He planned all your days on earth. Someday, your heart muscle will stop beating, and your body will die. That's part of God's plan too. But don't worry. You'll still be alive if you believe in Jesus' promise of forever life in heaven. If you've asked Him to forgive your sins and invited Him into your heart, your soul, that invisible "hidden heart" part of you, will leave your body and go to be with Jesus. In a heartbeat, you will be in heaven with Him and your loved ones who went before you. You will still be you, but any sin that made its way into your heart will be gone. You will finally be perfect, the way God created you to be. If you were afraid to die, that fear will be gone. In heaven, nothing bad can happen to you. Because heaven is forever, nothing will ever die. There is no sadness or worry there, only joy.

Heaven is a real place filled with real people. It's where God and Jesus live. God rules His heavenly kingdom from His throne surrounded by angels. We don't know much about what heaven looks like. It's far too wonderful for our earthly thoughts to imagine, but the Bible says it was designed and built by God. It is a city with buildings (Hebrews 11:10), and Jesus says there are many places to live there. He is already preparing a home for you (John 14:2). We don't know for sure what people do in heaven, but God gives each of us special talents and skills to use on earth, and we can imagine we will use them in heaven too.

Your body is young and will likely last a very long time. Right now, you are a girl living life on earth, and it is a wonderful life. Enjoy every minute because that's what God wants you to do. Love life and have fun! If you are worried about dying someday, don't be. Heaven is something in your future you can look forward to. Your wonderful life will never end—in heaven with God, it will only get better.

[Jesus said,] "For sure, I tell you, he who puts his trust in Me has life that lasts forever."
JOHN 6:47

Dear Jesus, thank You for Your promise of forever life in heaven. . .

SCRIPTURE INDEX